# *NELSON'S NOTES*

# *ON CHRISTIAN HISTORY*

## From New Testament Christianity to the Present Day

### Dr. Dan R. Nelson

# Dedication

I dedicate this work to my Mother and Father, who are now with the Lord.

In addition to having us in church so that I was converted to Christ early in my life, they fostered learning I could not have experienced in any normal home. They were both teachers and played an important role in my interest in History.

My Mother, Irma Lois Nelson, was my Fourth-Grade teacher. She had a book in my hand as a toddler and encouraged reading, opening the door to many possibilities in my life. She sponsored reading workshops that led to many incentives to read as much as I could. I tried to read anything I could get my hands on, particularly related to sports or History.

My Father was a head football coach and an American History teacher. I read almost everything related to the Civil War during the Centennial of the War Between the States. He had me come into his eleventh-grade American History Class and tell them all I knew about the Civil War when I was in the Fifth grade.

My Father always made History fun. In his History class, I remember him getting the eleventh graders to make replicas of the Monitor and Merrimack (The first ironclad ships battling in the Civil War). He always talked with me about History and my ancestors who fought in the Civil War. We traced their lives through relatives, and it was pretty easy on one Great-Great Grandaddy, who lived until 1929.

When I got to college and Seminary, my favorite course was History. I majored in Biblical Studies and History in college. In Seminary, I had a lot of classes on Church History, and my Ph.D. dissertation was on the Great Awakening preachers.

I have authored most of my Christian History books, primarily about the Baptist faith. My teachers in college and Seminary were also encouragers in Christian History. I have already dedicated my book *Baptist Biographies and Happenings* in American History to all my teachers in this area. I remember B.F. Smith at William Carey University, Jack Manning at Golden Gate Baptist Seminary, Claude Howe, and James Mosteller at New Orleans Baptist Seminary and their teachings with fondness.

To my parents and all the teachers who have influenced me and given me a thirst for Historical studies in any era, I am grateful and am still researching History. My quest is still alive because you have made my studies interesting and worthwhile.

# Endorsements

## By D Glenn Simmons, Ph.D., Th.D.

Dan Nelson's History of Christianity offers one of the most exhaustive overviews of how Christianity has impacted the world around it. His methodical, well-documented work is clearly a work I could easily recommend to my students, as well as to all the students of the History of Christianity at my University.

With a writing style that is clear and lucid, Dr. Nelson proceeds with accurate information on how Christianity impacted the world. Certainly, this well-documented and thoroughly researched work leaves no question as to its factual validity. The references are thorough and well-respected. He leaves no question as to the flow of the Church's 2000-year movement. I find the book interesting and intriguing. His depth and writing style often triggered responses from me that wanted to go off later and dig deeper. He gave me resources that I could use to do just that.

Without a doubt, I highly recommend this work. With years of experience in this field, Dr. Nelson brings a breadth and depth that few others have done. For the student of the Church, this is a must-read. He helps the reader put the actions of the Church into a proper historical perspective. This book is invaluable in understanding the Church's status and importance today."

D Glenn Simmons, Ph.D., Th.D.
Executive Director/Campus Dean
Professor of Christian Ministry & Counseling
Wayland Baptist University San Antonio

## By Steve Lemke, Provost Emeritus

Perhaps at no time in the Church's history have believers been so oblivious to our history. In this volume, Dan Nelson offers a readable history of the Christian church for laypersons. This work helps fill that significant void by sharing with current-day believers how believers through history have served the Lord

Steve Lemke, Provost Emeritus,
New Orleans Baptist Theological Seminary

## By David Lindow, Pastor

Dan Nelson's book on The History of Christianity, is an amazing accomplishment. I feel like he has placed an elephant in a matchbox. Getting 2000 years of Christian History in a 400-page book is close to a miracle. His book is fast-paced, moving quickly from one century to the next with consistent flashbacks to fit in all the details. He covers every major movement in Christianity and every major player as he progresses through the years. Anyone desiring a 20,000 feet view of the 2000 years of Christian History that includes many of the details without getting lost on rabbit hunts will not be disappointed.

David Lindow,
Pastor First Baptist Church of Universal City, Texas

## By Steve Miller, Pastor

Dr. Dan Nelson asks a Christian in his book concerning The History of Christianity: "Why should a Christian study history?" With clarity and credibility, Dan affirms the reason is the premise that Christianity is a historical faith. Not primarily ethical or philosophical but historical. This book is not revisionist history or telling us something new but is a simple yet bold reminder of what we need to remember referencing our Christian heritage. He leaves nothing out of importance for the reader. He details the challenges, the celebrations, and the conquering truth of the church and its characters. The book is understandable and will aid in teaching and individual growth. It will remind us as Christians that we are heirs of a great heritage.

Steve Miller
Former pastor of Missions
Chairman of Deacons
First Baptist Church of Universal City, Texas

# Table of Contents

# Introduction

What you have before you are a compilation of my History of Christianity notes that began over two decades ago. I taught at Channel Islands Bible College in Oxnard, California, and I put an outline together to guide and help my students. From that early and lean start, the notes kept growing. I expanded my class to two semesters since it is hard to cover the History of Christianity in one semester, no matter how much you must scale it down.

My early notes were personal because of my major in Church History in seminary and my double major in college, which covered Biblical Studies and the History of Christianity. My Ph.D. dissertation was on the Great Awakening Preachers, and my previous books have dealt with biographies of notable Baptist personalities. Even my books dealing with doctrine have approached beliefs from a historical perspective.

As I continued to expand my notes, I began to do more research from various Church Histories, which either confirmed or adjusted what I might have originally taught. After all these additions, I had a wealth of quotes from these sources and a different way of approaching various Histories that supported and confirmed what I had been teaching.

I share my journey in coming to this History before you to let you know that my writing is not just something I think or imagine about every event and personality I have given in this study.

My purpose is not to give you a study in Christian History that seems never-ending. Yet, my book is not a sparse mention of events and individuals who have left a mark in Christian History either.

The readers must put themselves in a situation to make this History personable and real. History should not be dull but exciting and earth-shattering.

Each chapter is loaded with individuals, events, trends, and happenings that have left a mark in our lives over 2,000 years since Jesus walked the earth and paid the ultimate price for the penalty of our sin. That great sacrifice resulted in His Resurrection and sending the disciples into the world with the greatest message one could ever hear.

My purpose in giving you this History of Christianity, among many, is for you to imagine what it was like to be in a certain period of history in an exciting way. Most of all, I want to help you see how history has shaped and brought us to where we are today.

My previous books have been well-documented and researched. I always tell people that my writing is the opposite of fiction novels. It does slow the process down but affirms and validates what you are writing.

I am grateful for all the History written about Christianity and desire this History to result in a sweeping understanding of Christian History, which people can access for valuable information. Like many sermons I have preached, may this history get a hold of something meaningful and helpfully shared for your life. I want to share this history so you can gain information and make it transferable and life-changing.

Often, I was inspired and motivated to serve God in pastoral and evangelistic pastoral ministry. I heard Dr. John Drakeford (a teacher then at Southwestern Baptist Theological Seminary) speak in a William Carey University chapel service while a student there. I was earnestly seeking God's will for a Seminary where I could study and serve where I was enrolled. Drakeford gave a biography of William Carey. It motivated me to hear Carey's sacrifices of leaving home forever and losing a wife and children on the mission field. If a man of such devotion went through all of these hardships to be "The Father of Modern Missions," I knew I could overcome any obstacle I might face in going West where the number of Christians was in the minority. I surmised that if he could make such sacrifices, I could go to California and leave my parents and brothers behind, as well as other relatives and the section of the country where I grew up. I went, and God blessed my pastoral and evangelistic ministry there for my entire ministerial career.

This History helps you gain facts and learn more about individuals and events. I pray it can be life-changing, motivating, and equipping you in whatever endeavor you undertake. This aspiration is my hopeful desire of what you can gain and comprehend in reading and studying this History that has evolved to be transformed into whatever God has for you to do with your life.

You can string all these events, movements, and individuals together. Some portions will be lean, while others will be full of the overflowing information I share. These facts and people may seem a little unbalanced. Still, they follow my expertise and knowledge in areas I have studied or lack knowledge regarding events I did not fully understand in previous studies.

The events and movements will be approached from my understanding and, at times, my opinions on these facts. I do not purpose to be 100% neutral. My studies and background will guide you, and you will be free to disagree. Yet, I will share why I believe a certain way concerning these matters.

Regarding individuals, you will read about heroes and villains. You will see the majority of these personages in the middle. I will not embellish or look for someone to prove my belief. Most of us will identify with someone or some period of Christian History. Through it all, I hope you will be challenged and inspired to follow God's will and allow Him to do great things through you as He has through certain individuals in Christian History.

May you gain understanding and be challenged to face whatever you face in opposition or reception like these heroes in Christian History did. May we constantly rely on the living God and the greatest message through the gospel of Christ for the world.

# Chapter 1

# The Apostolic Age 30-100

We will start with the growth of Christianity after the Great Commission given by Jesus in Matthew 28:19-20. I will not revisit Jesus's ministry leading to His atonement made for sin and his bodily resurrection. This great truth is the message on which we base our faith on what Christian History is all about.

We will study within the confines of the gospel message, which has been perverted through the centuries in many ways yet has survived as a central and definitive message throughout history that still changes lives.

That message is Jesus Christ, born of a virgin, God in human flesh, who lived a life without sin, died as a substitutionary sacrifice for our sin on the cross so that when we believe in His atoning work, God imputes His righteousness to us and sees us in Him. He rose bodily and visibly from the grave. Jesus ascended into heaven after authorizing His Church and sending them into the world with the gospel. He empowered them with the Holy Spirit and is returning to establish His kingdom on earth as in heaven.

The gospels are clear, and studies are given in many ways regarding Jesus' life on earth, prophesied, fulfilled, as the ultimate sacrifice for our sin, who is risen to live forever. This History deals with the effects of the gospel message on the world and how it changed everything from when He declared victory over the grave to His return to heaven with the promise of one day to return.

## A. The Strength of the Early Church

We are left with notable characteristics of the early Christians as they entered the world with the gospel message. They are:

1. The Message of the Gospel.

The Gospel is the greatest message in the world. Paul declared it by simplicity in I Cor. 15:3-4. It was not just an opinion or even a deep conviction the disciples and those following Jesus would have.

The message changed lives wherever the followers of Christ went. They saw people's lives saved and given meaning and purpose as they went everywhere with the gospel.

People voluntarily trusted in Christ as Savior. It was not socially acceptable to accept Christ, and they never coerced anyone into placing saving faith in Him.

The Philippian Jailer and his family is an example of such conversions. (Acts 16:31-34).

2. There was a worldwide expansion of the Christian movement

They were fulfilling the Great Commission in taking the gospel to the ends of the earth. The gospel crossed all cultural and geographic barriers. (Acts 1:8).

3. The Holy Spirit empowered the early Church at Pentecost

The disciples were not just lecturing on Jesus. They followed God's leading and saw His power to get strength in the face of martyrdom, as with Stephen, and the fortitude to face prison and execution, as with Peter and Paul.

The early Christians encountered the power and leadership of the Spirit wherever they went. Despite their inadequacies, God took over in many cases and many ways. This power was seen at Pentecost and throughout the book of Acts, prompting Peter to acclaim in Acts 12:15-17 *And as I began to speak, the Holy Ghost fell on them, as on us at the beginning.16 Then remembered I the word of the Lord, how that he said, John indeed baptized with water; but ye shall be baptized with the Holy Ghost.17 Forasmuch then as God gave them the like gift as he did unto us, who believed on the Lord Jesus Christ; what was I, that I could withstand God?* [1]

---

[1] All Biblical References are taken from the King James Version of the Bible, Zondervan: Grand Rapids, MI, 1994).

In this case, God's spirit overruled Peter's inclinations in leading Him to Cornelius' household, and they trusted Christ as Savior following Him in baptism.

### 4. The Commitment of Christ Followers

The early Christians took the gospel Everywhere. Bruce Shelley said, "First-century Christianity was a spiritual explosion ignited by the event in the presence of Jesus Christ; the Church hurdled in all directions, geographic as well as social."[2]

They were willing not only to suffer some but to die for the cause of Christ and be rewarded in heaven, as Stephen visualized in His stoning (Acts 7: 55-56).

Paul expressed it best when others tried to persuade Him not to go to Jerusalem and face events that would lead to his death when he said…" *for I am ready not to be bound only, but also to die at Jerusalem for the name of the Lord Jesus*" (Acts 23:11).

The early Christians went forward with fearless composure, even dying, if need be, for the cause of Christ.

### 5. The Extension of the Gospel

The early Christians shared the gospel and started churches, fulfilling Christ's intention for the world to receive His message. Restricting Himself

---

[2] Bruce L. Shelley, *Church History in Plain Language* (Word: Waco, TX, 1982), 41.

to one body, Jesus foresaw the day the gospel message would go forth and multiply His ministry and message throughout the world (John 14:12).

6. The Reception of the Gospel and its message to the World

People could be one in Christ, be equals, and find purpose and love for others. These results were a great contradiction to the stark message of hate and hostility in violent means to others. Now, people could be one in Christ. The gospel appealed to the masses by breaking down class barriers (Gal. 3:28).

## B. The Challenges of the Early Church

1. There were a variety of false teachings and the need for Doctrinal Clarification.

The epistles addressed specific Church problems and had particular messages for the Churches through them. Romans and Galatians – Justification by Faith; 1st and 2nd Corinthians – Personal Morality and Integrity; Ephesians –Our Position in Christ; Philippians –Rejoicing in Adversity; Colossians –Who Jesus is; 1st and 2nd Thessalonians -The Return of Christ; 1st and 2nd Timothy and Titus -How to lead a Church; Philemon –Forgiveness to others; Hebrews –What Jesus did and is doing today; James -Faith proved by works; 1st, 2nd, and 3rd John –trusting in the Real Jesus; Jude – Standing against false doctrine; Revelation – Comfort and future history.

A specific reference to combating false teaching, such as Gnosticism, is seen in I John 1:1-

2. John wrote to counter the false doctrine of Docetism that Jesus was a ghost and not physically present. Shelley says, "The title comes from the teaching that Christ was not really a man; he was a spectral appearance. He only seemed to suffer for man's sins since we all know divine phantoms are incapable of dying. This teaching continued throughout the first few centuries. Ignatius emphasized both Christ's deity and Christ's humanity." [3]

Ignatius reinforced the scriptural understanding of the true nature of Christ. He was an early spokesman for the deity of Christ. He said, "There is only one God, who is both flesh and spirit, born and unborn, God in man, true life and death, both from Mary and from God, the first subject to suffering and then beyond it, Jesus Christ our Lord."[4]

Ignatius also believed that faith in the unity of God was another essential component of oneness in the Christian community. Ignatius's emphasis on the importance of a common faith also made us sense Paul's words. Paul reminded the Ephesians Church of the "One Faith" (Eph 4:5).[5]

2. There was a Second Generation who had not been with Jesus.

These had not been with Jesus personally, so they naturally tended to be less excited than the

---

[3] Ibid. 65

[4] Jeffery Bingham, Pocket History of the Church, (University Press; Downers Grove, Il 2002), 25-26.

[5] Ibid

first generation. The beginning of persecution was a test to see if they would be as dedicated as the apostles and their generation.

### 3. Imperial Persecution by Rome Intensified

The persecution after Pentecost was scattered compared to how Rome treated the Christians under Nero. Peter and Paul were both martyred for their faith, probably in Rome. Christians were used as a sport in the arena, singled out in society as antagonists, and ridiculed for their faith. Many believers had to go underground for fear of mass slaughter.[6]

## C. The Dedication of Early Christians

### 1. They Refused to Worship Ceasar

These were some of the problems for Caesar and the Romans:

a. Truth against Error: They believed Caesar was a false God, and to worship him would be heresy and deny Christ.

b. Morality against Immorality: The worship of Caesar and acceptance of Roman culture involved many immoral practices that Christians refused entrapment into participating in these sins.

### 2. They were willing to die for their Faith

---

[6] jimkuo2, The Colosseum: Power, Brilliance, and Brutality (https://depts.washington.edu/hrome/Authors/jimkuo2/IlCo losseo/253/pub_zbpage_view.html#:~:text=Were%20Chris tians%20really%20fed%20to,in%20a%20less%20public%2 0place, Sept. 6, 2004, (Accessed October 23, 2024)

The sacrifice and dedication of its followers were amazing. Many believers died in the Coliseum or at the hands of the Romans when Nero turned against them. Very few renounced their faith and burned incense to Caesar. They were willing to die as believers rather than succumb to having their lives saved here by their worship of Caesar.

3. They brought a Christian Ethic into a Pagan Society

Christians stood out with their different morality and worship. Some may have viewed them scornfully, but others were changed by the life-giving message of the gospel. Justin Martyr expressed the ethics this way:

"Those who rejoiced in fornication now delight incontinence alone; those who made use of magic arts have dedicated themselves to the good and unbegotten God; we once took most pleasure in the means of increasing our wealth and property, now bring what we have into a common fund and share with everyone in need; we who hated and killed one another and would not associate with men of other tribes because of (their different) customs, now after the manifestation of Christ live together and pray for our enemies."[7]

The change brought to lives and their witness was truly noticeable and investigated even with the opposition against the early Christian message.

The courage of early believers did much to change the world as Jesus had commanded. From

---

[7] Bingham, 34

such small beginnings with just common people, the Christian message shared everywhere gained momentum. Despite persecution, the Roman Empire would not kill the message even though they killed many messengers. The Christian faith headed toward transforming lives and, eventually, a culture.

# Chapter 2

# Persecutions, Heresies, and Spokesmen of Christianity in the Roman Empire 100-312

Persecution did not let up for the early Christians, but the blood of the martyrs became seeds of hope and help in a world that did not know the true message of Christ. Their enemies and those who were passive about them were about to learn about it; however, when they saw their dedication and heard the gospel, they stood up and took notice.

Heresies began to slip their way into the Christian movement. When they started to veer off from the true message, strong men stood against them with the truth of God's Word and the Christian message. The age for defenders of the faith and apologists evolved. Defenders of the truth continue today. Where there is truth, there will always be errors seeking to oppose it.

These spokesmen for the truth filled the gap before the final canon of Scripture was accepted. Christians were not ashamed of the truth they expressed in their writings and their strong stands for God's truth.

# A. The most Severe Times of Persecution

### 1. Why they Suffered Persecution

There were specific misunderstandings and just plain lies told against early believers, designed to make them enemies of the state. Shelley describes:

" Pagans concluded that Christians must be eating and drinking human flesh and blood by observing Jesus' words, 'This bread is my body. This cup is my blood.' . . . . the charge of gross immorality came from the fact that one Christian meeting was called the Agape – the Love Feast – and from the custom of the 'holy kiss' of peace the Christians gave to one another."[8]

One of the most famous stories of early Christian martyrs was Polycarp, the pastor of the Church in Smyrna. He was John's disciple, who became Bishop of Smyrna and was burned at the stake at age 92. Christians were called atheists because they did not believe in the Roman gods and refused to burn incense before an altar or image of the emperor, making him a god.

---

[8] Shelley, 57

Polycarp's interchange with the proconsul is an interesting statement of faith and testimony of the courage of early Christians. When asked to recant his faith, Polycarp answered, "I have served Him (Christ) eighty-six years, and He has done me no wrong; how can I blaspheme the King who saved me?" The proconsul tried once more; "Swear by the genius of Caesar." Polycarp replied simply, "I am a Christian." The proconsul threatened to throw him to the beasts. Polycarp answered, "Bring them in." The magistrate menaced him with fire, but Polycarp counseled him that the fire which burns for an hour is not to be compared to the fire of eternal punishment, and he was then burned to death.[9]

Polycarp's death (even as an older man) indicated the courage and boldness of their leaders and all Christians who were not afraid to stand for their Lord. To die for their faith was just a way for God to take them home. They did not have a death wish but looked to the Lord Jesus Christ, who had warned them not to fear what man could do to them (Matt 5:11-12, 10:18-20).

2. How they were Persecuted

Christians were used as a sport in the Coliseum and fed to lions, burned in Nero's gardens for pleasure, and many other hideous practices inflicted upon them. Foxes' Book of Martyrs explains in detail many of these hideous persecutions:

---

[9] Roland Bainton, *Christendom; a Short History of Christianity and its Impact on Western Civilization*, Volume I From the Birth of Christ to the Reformation, 1964 (Harper & Roe: New York), 63.

"The courage of the early believers was evident in their witness and captured in some of their spokesman's writings. Ignatius typified the attitude of many Christians martyred as he was; he wrote in a letter to the Romans, "I am writing to all the Churches and am insisting to everyone that I die for God of my own free will – unless you hinder me. I implore you not to be 'unseasonably kind' to me. Let me be the food for the wild beasts; then I will truly be a disciple of Jesus Christ when all the world no longer sees my body."[10]

This testimony revealed the fearlessness of many of the early believers.

There were periods of relative peace (not completely peaceful but tolerable) and tremendous persecution. The last severe persecution of Christians came in 303 under Emperor Diocletian, requiring that all Church buildings be destroyed and all copies of Scriptures consigned to be publicly burned. Christians lost their civil status and protection of laws.[11] This all-out war on the Christians did not deter them from worshipping God, standing for and sharing the message of the gospel.

At times, emperors used the persecution of Christians to their advantage. They blamed them for crimes they did not commit and were innocent of. Lies were told about them "to pass the buck, so to speak." To turn hatred away from Nero burning

---

[10] Foxe, John, 1516-1587. Fox's Book of Martyrs, or, The Acts and Monuments of the Christian Church, J.B. Smith: Philadelphia :1856.
[11] Bainton, Vol, 1, 89

Rome, he accused the Christians of having set the fire in 64 A.D. The accusation was certainly not true, but large numbers of Christians were arrested. Terrible persecution followed. Many Christians were even crucified; some were sown up in skins of wild beasts; then big dogs let loose upon them and torn to pieces. Women were tied to mad bulls and dragged to death.

Nero found cruel ways to persecute and kill Christians. After nightfall, Christians were burned at the stake in Nero's Garden. The Roman people who hated the Christians were free to come into the garden, and Nero drove around in his chariot, enjoying the horrible spectacle to the full.[12] Such displays of cruelty threatened to silence and kill the Christian movement. Yet, even giving the ultimate sacrifice for their faith did not stop them.

3. When They were persecuted

Nero's persecution was only the beginning of killing Christians. Christians were used as easy targets of blame and misrepresentations. They were persecuted and murdered by a long line of emperors. The emperor and date for these persecutions were as follows: Persecutions: Nero 62, Domitian 90, Trajan 112, Decius 250, Diocletian 290, Galerius 311.[13] These were not the only times of persecution,

---

[12] Shelley, 56

[13] Mark Galli, "Persecution in the Early Church," Christian History Institute, https://christianhistoryinstitute.org/magazine/article/persecution-in-early-church-gallery, 1990, (Accessed, January, 21, 2025).

but these were periods of extreme persecution and, at times, brutality against them.

Difficult tests forced Christians to stand up for Christ or deny Him. Under Emperor Decius, 200-251, Caesar worship described was made universal, compulsory for every nation within the empire except the Jews. Caesar worship described gives a picture of what Christians were up against:

On a certain day of the year, every Roman citizen had to come to the Temple of Caesar, burn a pinch of incense there, and say, "Caesar is Lord." After a man had burned his incense pinch and acknowledged Caesar as lord, he could go away and worship any God he'd like, so long as that worship did not affect public decency and order. Thus, we see that Caesar worship described was primarily a test of political loyalty; it was a test of whether or not someone was a good citizen.[14]

Citizenship being tied to the denial of Christ by the worship of Caesar was a severe test and a brutal forcing of Christians to reveal themselves as believers loyal to Caesar or Christ.

## B. Heresies afflicting Early Christianity

If Christians and churches were not destroyed externally, there was heresy internally that was a threat and danger to the true faith they held. These heresies were labeled and persuaded by some but were challenged by spokesmen for the early Christians.

---

[14] Ibid, 59

1. Regarding the Person of Christ

a. Gnosticism: This heresy said Christ was created, not God, and believed matter was evil, so they did not believe Jesus had a fleshly body.[15] This view made him a spirit and a lesser being than God. Colossians and 1st John attacked this heresy (I John 4:1-3).

b. Monophysitism: Led by Eutyches, It said Christ's divine nature was so evident that his human nature wasn't seen. He made Jesus God only and not man.[16]

c. Nestorianism: Led by Nestorius, Jesus was a man who became half God and half man.[17]

d. Apollinarianism said Christ was purely God and only used a human body. Apollinarianism is similar to Modalism, believing only God the Father interchanged forms when he appeared as God.[18] This teaching made Christ a quick-change artist

2. Extra-Biblical Modalism

a. Montanism: Montanus led this heresy. He believed in extra personal revelation as given to him by God. He thought he was a prophet of the new age and rejected the Old Testament and Christ as divine.[19] Montanus's revelations became more important than the written word and had a more exalted position than the Scripture. The choice of

---

[15] Bingham, 40-41
[16] Ibid, 54-55
[17] Ibid, 51
[18] Ibid
[19] Shelley, 80-81

personal revelation over Scripture is a feature even today in many religious circles.

b. Marcion: He was a leading Gnostic who rejected most of the Old Testament. He did not accept Jesus as divine but looked to Paul and his views about the ethical teachings of Christianity.[20]

## C.  Spokesmen for Christianity

1. Clement of Rome (?-97) He was the Bishop of Rome who wrote from 96 to 98 letters to the Corinthian Church encouraging them to the unity of faith and practice of humility. He was not the Pope, as Catholicism has espoused. He was probably a bishop appointed by one of the apostles.[21]

2. Ignatius of Antioch (35-107) He was an early martyr of the Church who wrote letters from Rome before he was martyred for his belief in the Deity and humanity of Christ. He also encouraged other believers to suffer for their faith.

Ignatius was one of the first bishops to use the term Catholic Church. This designation, used at the end of the second century, continued to identify all Christians. "The designation widely used of the Church in the sense that the Catholic Church was both universal, in contrast to local congregations, and orthodox compared to heretical groups."[22] The Catholic designation did not refer to an organized, universal entity to which all believers in Christ were

---

[20] Ibid, 78-70
[21] Bingham 20-21
[22] Shelley, 42

subservient. The terminology never replaced the local congregations, describing local bishops leading a local congregation. True New Testament Churches existed as independent, separate bodies with no Ecclesiastical heads.

Ignatius was the Church pastor at Antioch and wrote a series of letters. In these, he spoke habitually of a single bishop (or pastor) in each Church, a body of presbyters and company of deacons. He said, "God's grace and the Spirit's power, he teaches, flow to the flock through this united ministry.[23] The congregations were united but not controlled by a universal entity.

3. Polycarp (70-155) He was the bishop of Smyrna and was John's disciple. His martyrdom (already described) is one of the most famous of the period and gives a firsthand picture of the dedication of the early Christians

4. Justin Martyr (100-165) He was a leading apologist of Christians. His first apology, written about 150, gave *A Defense for Christianity* and spoke to Christians about being separate from the world. Yet, he still believed Christians should not be isolated from the pagan world.[24]

Martyr was an apologist for the early Church. He studied as a Stoic, Pythagorean, and Platonist. None of these satisfied his yearning for spiritual reality. A stranger encouraged him to study the

---

[23] Ibid
[24] Ibid, 77

Jewish prophets. After reading the Scripture, Justin became a Christian.

Martyr also spoke of the evolution of the day of worship from Saturday to Sunday in Christian circles. He said, "On the day, called the Day of the Sun, all who live in cities or the country gather together to one place, and the memoirs of the apostles or the writings of the prophets are read, as long as time permits; . . . the president verbally instructs, and exhorts the imitation of these good things."[25] This window into the time for worshipping in early Churches is helpful to prove that the appropriated day of gathering to worship was not the Jewish sabbath but the day commemorating Jesus' Resurrection.

5. Irenaeus (120-200) He opposed the Gnostics by explaining to the Christian community the proper "fit" of Scripture in light of the Church's traditional teachings passed down by the apostles to the bishops. Irenaeus taught his congregation what the Church had taught before the Gnostics showed up. He appreciated the strength that resulted from a healthy union between Scripture and tradition.

Irenaeus pointed to the Church of Rome as the pre-eminent example, founded by the two martyred apostles, Peter and Paul, by the end of the second century. Three sources of authority had emerged: the canon, the creed, and oral tradition." Irenaeus led this movement to establish Church

---

[25] Ibid

authority.[26] The canon of Scripture was not a jumbled mess, but the writings and teachings were passed down to their present-day with careful consideration.[27]

6. Athenagoras (2nd Century) He wrote similarly in *his Plea for Christians*, 177, as he contrasted Christian conduct with the conduct accepted and even honored by Rome. He was also an apologist with a school of reason for explaining the Christian faith to others. This expectation encouraged all believers to give a good witness to those who misunderstood them.[28]

7. Clement of Alexandria (150-211) Clement appropriated Greek culture to describe the education of the Christian. Education needed in light of the Christian message spreading worldwide became a great need.[29]

8. Tertullian (155-220) He was an apologist to the Romans for Christians who coined the phrase "The Trinity". His *Apology* underlined the legal and moral absurdity of the persecution directed against Christians. Some of his other books were an encouragement to those facing martyrdom. He attacked the heretics, explained the Lord's Prayer and the meaning of baptism, and helped develop

---

[26] Ibid, 86
[27] Bingham, 41
[28] Paul Pavo, *Christian History for Everyman*: "Athenagoras" https://www.christian-history.org/athenagoras.html, 2014, (Accessed November 7, 2024).
[29] Bainton, Vol 1, 79

the orthodox understanding of the Trinity.[30] Through this understanding of Christ's true nature, he could help others to stand against false teachings that robbed Him of His deity. [31]

9. Origen (185-253) He is known for spiritualizing the Scripture. He saw allegories in Scripture, learned from Clement, and was the first to express belief in purgatory. Although he studied the Scripture diligently and explained it, he was on the borderline of being a heretic in that he spiritualized hell, the devil, and other important teachings of the Scripture. These specific beliefs did not line up with Scripture.

Origen had a vision in which he saw all creatures, including the devil himself, being restored to communion with God one day. Hell would be emptied. The doctrine, above all others, caused him no end of trouble. Origen's error lay in turning a dream into a doctrine. His belief may have been the first teaching that later Catholicism used to justify Purgatory.[32]

Origen was also a leader of the Alexandrian School of Theology. They emphasized the divine nature of Christ more than his human nature. Origen was the first to coin the term "God/Man" to describe Jesus Christ.[33] It was a true designation,

---

[30] Shelley, 48
[31] Ibid, 48
[32] Ibid, 101
[33] Ibid, 124

but one could not deny His humanity being a full man and God.

10. Eusebius (260-339) Eusebius recorded much of early Christian History for the first 350 years. Many people who claimed to speak for the Church brought pagan philosophy with them into the Church, as Eusebius documents. Without his History, we would have little information about the spokesman and leaders of early Christianity.[34]

These spokesmen have been called the "Church Fathers." They were the fathers of the truth, ensuring the Christian faith and its truths not be taken for granted. They were also the spokesman of the truth, leading to Christianity engulfing the Roman empire and its influence living on forever.

---

[34] Ibid, 116-117

# Chapter 3

# The Constantine Era 312-490

One might feel that the Constantine era was a tremendous boon for Christians. Certainly, the end of persecution was a welcome realization. However, mistakes were made by the emperor, and the universal acceptance of the empire to Christianity without a lack of understanding of how one becomes an individual committed to Christ was a problem.

The good that came from accepting Christianity helped articulate the faith in the Council of Nicaea and other Councils that would follow.

The Holy Land was rediscovered, and certain sites commemorated, marking the places where Jesus ministered. The era was one of mixed blessings, but the good that came from it was one of the blessings God provided.

# A. The Conversion of Constantine

1. Constantine was engaged in a Civil War with Galerius and Maxentius.

He wanted to appease the growing Christian population, which was becoming more vocal. This appeasement was a worthy goal with the Christians still alive and living in the empire. It also was a good political move to ingratiate himself with everyone.

2. Constantine embraced Christianity.

He saw a heavenly vision of the cross and said he had become a Christian. He heard a voice that said, "By this sign, conquer."[35] The reported vision led to controversy over whether it was an actual cross or a vision.

3. Constantine wins the Civil War

A civil war ensued between Constantine and Maxentius. Maxentius was hostile toward Christians, and "Constantine took the astounding step of announcing his conversion to the Christian religion."[36] His "conversion" was more of an endorsement of Christianity, and his true acceptance of Christ as Savior had been and will continue to be a question.

4. Constantine was baptized on his Deathbed

This last episode of Constantine's life has questioned his surety of being a true follower of Christ. He believed baptism washed away all

---

[35] Bainton, Vol. 1, 91
[36] Ibid, 91

previous sins and was already adopting the Church's evolution to baptismal regeneration. Many believe he didn't have a total understanding of Christianity and salvation.[37]

## B. The Edict of Milan and its Impact

1. Constantine decreed Christianity as the Official State Religion in 313.

The decree itself was impossible to observe because one is not made a Christian by decree but by trusting in Christ's sacrifice for us personally and by repenting from sin. The Edict of Milan stopped all discrimination against Christians and adopted Christianity as the State Religion. Frank Meade said:

"After three hundred years of uncertainty, terror, and persecution, they were free to come up out of their caves and their catacombs and set up their altars where they chose to worship God in the sunlight, in the Forum, in the street. They could build their Churches above ground, meet, pray, and read the Scriptures without fear of arrest or pagan gibe. They could accept public office; their clergy would rank with the priests of Apollo and Genetrix; their ecclesiastical courts would be recognized. At the stroke of a pen or a quill, they were lifted from ridicule to respectability."[38]

2. Constantine enforced Christianity as the State Religion.

------

[37] Meade Frank, The Ten Decisive Battles of Christianity. (Bobbs-Merrill, Co: New York, 1936), 49
[38] Meade, 47

He made all citizens embrace Christianity and built a capital at Constantinople in the East.[39] Think of it: In one decree, all citizens were said now to be Christians, all pagan priests, Christian priests, and all pagan gods to be subservient to the Christian's God. But it is not that easy. Conversion by degree cannot be attained that easily.

3. Constantine called the First Great Church Council at Nicaea.

Constantine tried to promote Christianity and call for clarification of its beliefs in the first, possibly the most important council. The first meeting was held in 318 and featured maimed and injured Christian leaders coming to Nicaea and working with the emperor in a "Christian Kingdom." The council clarified the doctrine and offered a confession in 325. Christianity now had the freedom it needed but, in the process, lost its true significance through gradual compromise.[40] The council's confession has come to be known as the Nicaean Creed.

## C.  Changes Made by Constantine

1. The Division of the Empire

The Eastern Empire became more of a religiously structured society with new churches, such as Saint Sophia's Cathedral, built by the emperor, Theodosius. Also, the Eastern Empire allowed the Roman Church to be closer to the Holy Land, which would become more important later in

---

[39] Shelley, 109
[40] Meade, 50-51

the Crusades era. The establishment of the Eastern Empire allowed it to have more of a Christian emphasis since it started afresh and didn't deal with the renouncement of the pagan gods of the Romans.

2. The Eastern Empire and its Influences

a. The Theodosian Era: By 380, rewards for Christians had given way to penalties for non-Christians. That year, Emperor Theodosius (340-395) made belief in Christianity a matter of imperial command. He said, "It is our will that peoples we rule shall practice that religion which the divine Peter the Apostle transmitted to the Romans." Theodosius took for granted the close link between his will and God's. He instituted strict policies for breaking the day of worship and moral guidelines that enforced Christianity as a State Religion. So strict was Theodosius in his enforcement of Christianity that Ambrose of Milan (Augustine's teacher) reproved him. He denied communion until he confessed his sin.[41] Anyone seeing the change of the empire to Christianity was probably shocked. The changes came after a generation realized that paganism was gone and had no past false gods to contend with.

b. The Justinian Code: Emperor Justinian (482-565) also developed a code based on the ethic of Christianity and was a model for governments that would use the Christian ethic to enforce wrongdoing. Through this code of conduct, one could see what a true Christian looked like and

---

[41] Shelley, 111-112

identified. It was more a code to live by. Bainton shared, "It began with a section on the Holy Trinity and included rules governing the qualifications of bishops. Moreover, it penalized religious dissenters. Against heretics, it repeated the penalties of the earlier Theodosian Code passed by emperor Theodosius, inflicting the death penalty on those who denied the Trinity, such as the Arians, and those who repeated baptism as the Donatists.[42] This enforcement of the original code now favored Christians and wrongly enforced such stringent penalties.

c. Differences in the Eastern and Western Church: There were differences in belief and practice between the Churches in the East and West. These differences distinguished the Western Church from the Eastern Church. "The Western Church had a central leader that, in time, was empowered to be infallible, called the Pope. The Eastern Church had a patriarch who had influence but did not have the Pope's power. The Western Church did not use icons the way the Eastern Church did. The architecture of its Churches was different, and the Eastern Churches' teachings were basically orthodox in that they did not insist on a strict sacramental system of salvation. However, it did refer to communion and baptism as sacraments. While Western Churches saw salvation through the Church and the ministry of the sacraments."[43] These sacraments would later become a source of confusion and elevation for

---

[42] Bainton, Vol.1, 111, 103
[43] Bingham, 45, 49

one's salvation in a departure from the teaching of Scripture.

Constantinople was overrun in the 1400s by Muslims, and the Western Church has endured to this day.[44] Closer proximity to the Holy Land made the Eastern Empire capital more vulnerable to attack and capture by the Muslim armies.

Now, on both fronts of the empire, Christianity was represented as a friend and not an enemy of the government. The understanding of the faith was clearer through some personalities that articulated the faith and preserved its great truths about Christ. The Councils would lead to a general acceptance of clear and certain books of the New Testament. Through this understanding, the completed Scripture has endured to this present day.

---

[44] Shelley, 168

# Chapter 4

# The Purpose of the Councils to the Christian Movement 318-778

The Councils helped define the Christian faith, especially as it pertained to the person and work of Christ. One can read the Scripture and know the stories of Christ's ministry, but to focus on His nature and work was continual in the several councils that finalized what the Scripture says about Christ. The heresies continued, but the clarity that the councils brought and the continued group of scholars helped many to understand these great truths.

One factor, though, was the power of Catholicism, as it began with the first universal acceptance of a Pope. Now, power has started to increase, and the power of State Religion has helped fortify this power.

One of the outcomes of the Council era was how it defined Scripture to those who were illiterate and could not read or fully understand the message of the Bible. The problem we shall see is the enforcement power the Church developed through all-powerful rulers gave them such power.

## A.  The Major Councils

The person of Christ was the first theological issue the Councils met and needed for the Christian understanding of the full identity of Jesus.

Shelley describes the issue that necessitated the council:

"The most troublesome dispute in the east centered in Alexandria, where Arius, pastor of the influential Bausalis Church, came into conflict with his bishop, Alexander. Sometime around 318, Arius openly challenged teachers in Alexandria by asserting that the word (logos) to assume flesh in Jesus Christ (John 1:14) was not true God and that he had an entirely different nature, neither eternal nor omnipotent. To Arius, when Christians called Christ God, they did not mean He was deity, except in an approximate sense. He was a lesser being, or half God, not the eternal and changeless creator. . . Arius' views were very popular because he had an eloquent preaching style."[45]

Different views of the nature of Christ called for a unified understanding concerning His nature. Constantine called for the Council of Nicaea to address the issue of the nature of Christ. The

---

[45] Shelley, 114

expression that came from this Council was the Latin (homo ousion); one substance was probably introduced by Bishop Hosius of Cordova (in today's Spain). This description identified Jesus as God in the flesh in a different manifestation than the Father and of one substance with the Father, which came out of the Nicaean Creed.[46] This statement clarified who Jesus is and stood against the attempt to define Him wrongly.

These conclusions of Christ were expressed:

1. Nicaea 325 Christ was fully divine. It looked at the Scripture canon and established the Nicene Creed.

2. Constantinople 381 Christ was fully human.

3. Ephesus 431 Christ was a unified person. Several heresies addressed in the Council of Ephesus answered their false claims.

a. Eutyches taught Monophysitism. He combined the two natures of Christ absorbed by the divine one.

Nestorius said that Jesus was divided between human and divine.

c. Arius denied the deity of Christ.

d. The Ephesus Council's Pronouncements:

The Council at Ephesus, against Arius, affirmed that Jesus was truly God; against Apolinarius, who only believed in the divine nature,

---

[46] Ibid, 115-116

affirmed that he was also truly man. Apolinarius also taught that Jesus was only divine and not truly human, similar to early Gnosticism. Against Eutyches, he confessed Jesus' deity and humanity were not changed into something else, and against Nestorius, that Jesus was not divided but one person.[47]

4. Chalcedon 451 The deity of Christ explained in greater detail supported His full divine and human nature. Christ was human and divine in one person. The Council of Chalcedon rejected the false teaching of Apollinaris, Nestorius, and Eutyches. It emphasized the oneness of Christ in his full two natures, divine and human, in unity with each other.[48]

## B. The Process of Biblical Canonization

Canon means rule, staff, or measuring rod. This word appropriately described the New Testament's fully inspired and accepted books.

1. The Council at Hippo 393

It published the final canon of Scripture, and the Council at Carthage 397 published the same list, promoting uniformity throughout the Christian world concerning the canon of Scripture.[49] These two councils finalized the acceptance of the canon of the New Testament, as we have it.

---

[47] Ibid, 128-129
[48] Latourette, Vol. 1, 171-172
[49] Shelley, 83

2. Influences

Athanasius was a strong proponent of the 27 books of the New Testament that we have today. Writings that did not reflect the message or the gospel of Christ were omitted and writings that were in common usage and traced back to the apostle's doctrine were accepted.[50] [51]

Athanasius *Festal Epistle* of 367 is commonly regarded as the first pronouncement defining the canon of the New Testament, which consists of those twenty-seven books it is now composed. Athanasius' approval of the accepted books today was very important because of his standing, study, and knowledge of the original text.[52]

3. The Scriptures were determined in three ways:

a. The uniqueness of the message presenting Christ: The oral tradition of the apostles was codified and made into written books. The writings answered the questions of the critics and the second generation of Christians.

b. A book's use in worship by local Churches: The Church leaders also accepted them at the time.

Eusebius had three categories: accepted, disputed, and spurious.

---

[50] Rich Martinez, "The Canon of the New Testament" https://www.biblicaltheology.com/Research/MartinezR01.html, 2002, (Accessed November, 5. 2024).
[51] Shelley, 83
[52] Martinez, Canon of the New Testament

There were Gnostic books, and Marcion pushed for their acceptance. The books were rejected because they needed to present Christ, His redemptive work, and his divine nature.

c. A book was tied to an apostle: Its validity found much credence if it had been written by an apostle or a companion who accompanied them.[53] These measures showed a good understanding of what books should be in the Bible as approved books.

# C. Major Theologians in the Era of the Councils

### 1. Athanasius (297-373)

A strong spokesman for the deity of Jesus Christ and the final canon of the New Testament. He battled Arius, a priest who did not believe Jesus was fully God but a created individual. Athanasius countered Arius' arguments through various writings and a creed that has come to be known as the *Athanasius Creed*. He was banished five times from the kingdom, but eventually, his view won acceptance in the Councils as it related to who Jesus was concerning his divine and human nature.

In his first work on The Incarnation, Athanasius developed from Scripture the key understanding of salvation as humanity's recreation to the death and resurrection of Jesus Christ, the Word of God. Through His death, the incarnate

---

[53] Bainton, Vol. 1, 69

(human) Word took on himself humanity's God-appointed destiny of defeat by death.

A second writing of Athanasius worth noting is his *Against the Arians*. One argument from this important work stands out: God alone can initiate and accomplish salvation. Therefore, the Word of God, who became flesh, could not be a creature; as Arius asserted, He must be one substance with the Father. *Athanasius' Against the Arians* is a classic rebuttal to Arianism.[54] His rebuttal was convincing and scriptural. It gave a good understanding of the true nature of Christ as revealed in the Bible.

Athanasius disputed the Arians under Arius. "He was only a deacon and secretary to the Bishop of Alexandria when he began to write against their teachings. Athanasius affirmed that man's eternal salvation is imperiled if the relationship of the Son to the Father is not eternal and unchangeable. Behind this view, Athanasius taught the belief held earlier by Irenaeus that humanity and divinity are not disparate and incapable of conjunction; the incarnation of God in Christ is proof. Christ is fully human, fully eternal, and unchangeably divine."[55] Athanasius' response was helpful and instructive in determining believers who believed the truth about Jesus' true nature.

2. John Chrysostom (347-407)

A famous preacher in the Eastern Empire did much to establish his pulpit ministry and believed in a strong pastoral ethic for those who were called into

---

[54] Bingham, 47-49
[55] Bainton, Vol. 1, 97-98

Christian ministry. He was known as the "Golden-Tongued Orator" of the Eastern Empire. He was an influential leader among Eastern Christians, even challenging Emperor Theodosius at one time in his directives as the Emperor of the Eastern Empire.[56] Chrysostom was convincing and earnest in his preaching, which affected many.

3. Augustine (354-430)

The Bishop of Hippo expressed much of the beliefs of the early churches. He expressed strong views on God's grace and original sin.

The famous leader had a dramatic conversion experience after living an immoral life as a youth. He recounted this experience in his book, *The Confessions of Augustine*. Later, he became an apologist for Christian influence in government and society in writing his classic work, *The City of God*. In this work, Augustine also tried to answer skepticism related to why Rome was vulnerable to outside attacks from foreign invaders.[57] Augustine believed since the fall, humanity has been in bondage to sin and has no freedom from either sinning or from experiencing its penalties, ultimately including death.

The monk Pelagius (350-425), whose teachings were influential during the first twenty years of the fifth century, strongly opposed

---

[56] Bradley Nassif John Chrysostom: The Golden-Mouth Preacher https://www.equip.org/articles/john-chrysostom-the-golden-mouth-preacher/ Aug 27, 202, (Accessed November 6, 2024).
[57] Bainton Vol. 1, 121-122, 126

Augustine's views. According to Pelagius, humans could choose their own destiny because they had free will and were not chained to inevitable sin. According to Augustine, God decreed the salvation of the human; a person experienced salvation because God decided to save him or her.[58] The sovereignty of God was in full sway over Augustine's theology.

Augustine was born to a pagan father and a Christian mother, Monica. He was reared as a Christian but not baptized. He came to Christ after living an immoral life as a youth and reading Romans 13:14, which says, "Put you on the Lord Jesus Christ and make no provision for the flesh." He heard a voice telling him to do that. He had a remarkable conversion experience in this way.

Before Augustine's conversion, he studied in Carthage and embraced the Creed of the Manichaeans, a religion of Persian origin. They were more extreme than the Gnostics and condemned matter as evil. After Augustine became a believer, he viewed man as having a sin nature inherited by birth. This sin nature was only overcome through the indwelling of the Holy Spirit in a person's life. Augustine had already encoun-tered Neoplatonism, which is the absence of good in a person's life. Still, this teaching ignored the nature of sin. After studying the book of Romans, Augustine was convinced that man has a sin nature that can only be overcome through the salvation experience by God's grace.

---

[58] Bingham, 110

Augustine became the Bishop of Hippo and published some of the most famous writings of all Christianity. His *Confessions of Augustine* relate to his salvation experience; his *City of God* later explains the reason why God allows evil and, even in the fall of Rome, justified war in defense of the barbarians. Augustine also believed in a strong central Church that would guard the truth and be the authority for scriptural teaching. His primary contribution is his view of the "doctrines of grace." This teaching was set against the teachings of Pelagius, who believed that the cooperation of good works with God saves sinners.

Augustine believed that only God's grace could redeem us from the penalty of sin, which is our inheritance through original sin. John Calvin later defined his doctrine during the Reformation.[59] Augustine's theology came to fruition under Calvin's teaching.

Augustine spoke against the Donatists, whose leader, Donatus (313-335), protested Catholic practices. Donatus felt that certain Catholic bishops had compromised the Scriptures, even handing them over to be burned during the last persecution under Diocletian. He called for a pure Church, not a mixed Church of the world and Church. Augustine said the Church must be a mixed multitude, and both good and bad people are in it as a reality.

Pelagius fought Augustine's theology with vigorous opposition against him. The monk denied that human sin is inherited from Adam and that man

---

[59] Bainton, Vol 1, 122-129

can act righteously or sinfully. Moreover, death is not a consequence of Adam's disobedience. Adam indeed introduced sin into the world, but only by his corrupting example and not through nature.

Augustine later coined "the doctrines of grace" (as mentioned), stating that "Sin is inherent to every generation and every person. God does predestine those who will be saved or have foreknowledge related to this and that death is the result of the corruption of sin in our lives. God's grace, through faith in Christ alone, can save us from this predicament of our corrupting sin nature."[60] Augustine and Pelagius confronted one another's teachings with great vigor.

Now, the developments in theology and teaching led to the acceptance of the final canon of our present-day Bible. Acceptance of most books has been prevalent since the time of Christ and the early churches that came from them. The official canon has gained universal acceptance through meticulous verification and is handed down to this present day.

We are still discussing and debating the views of Augustine and its opposition from Pelagius. The debate over predestination and free will continues in denominations and different groups that hold to either the views they had or maybe a mixture of both.

---

[60] Shelley, 141-145

# Chapter 5

# The Power of the Holy Roman Empire 600-1000

The Pope was recognized in the Western Empire and most of the civilized world. Rome's power in the spiritual realm increased as the power of the secular realm decreased. As the secular empire collapsed, the power of Catholicism was massive. The secular empire was beholden to the Pope and the "Universal Church." When the secular empire fell, the spiritual empire kept going.

The "Church" found new allies with the conversion of other secular rulers to Christianity. The most notable one was in the Kingdom of the Franks, where the supposed conversion of Charles Martel, Pepin, and Charlemagne occurred. A new distinction of the Holy Roman Empire protected the Church and installed Charlemagne as its first emperor. The "Church" took a giant step forward with this territory and position.

# A.  The Purpose of the Holy Roman Empire

1. Solidify the Power of the Church

The Holy Roman Empire gave power to the Church because of its protection and alliances that strengthened the Papacy.

2. Protection of the Vatican

The Donatists led opposition to the Bishop of Carthage through their leader, Donatus. They opposed the Bishop of Rome and felt he should not make all decisions for Christians worldwide. This resistance was the first opposition to Papal authority.[61] The Holy Roman Empire ensured the Papacy's freedom to oppose enemies with the backing of a civil ruler sworn to protect the Church.

3. Evolution of Power from the State to the Church

Papal power reached its height with Pope Innocent III (1198-1216). Innocent III claimed that even kings and nobles derived their authority from the Pontiff. Not all rulers recognized or submitted to this view, and the disagreements between some royals and Popes make for some of the most intriguing stories in Medieval History.[62] Innocent's expectation of civil authorities resulted from papal power's elevation through the

---

[61] Bainton, Vol. 1, 96-97
[62] Bingham, 90

centuries. The civil rulers supported the power grab through their military power and the reward from the Church for their support.

## B.  The Reign of Charlemagne

1. The Family of Charlemagne leading to his Reign

a. Pepin's conversion came through Boniface, a missionary sent out by Augustine. He was instrumental in the conversion of the King to Christianity. Pepin, in turn, made the Frankish Empire a Christian nation with allegiance to the Pope and to the Universal Church.[63] In a sense, Pepin duplicated Constantine's actions.

b. Charles Martel (known as the Hammer): Martel protected Europe from Muslim invaders in the Battle of Tours 720 A.D.[64] His defense of Europe and the Church brought the Church into league with his kingdom.

c. Pepin the Short Popes made alliances with Kings, and the Kings, in turn, protected Rome from invaders like the Lombards. The Kings deeded land to the Church, such as the "Donation of Pepin."[65] Pepin followed in his father's footsteps with his generous donation and church protection.

d. Charles the Great (742-814): He defeated his enemies and protected Europe and Rome from invaders. Charles the Great (Charlemagne)

---

[63] Bainton, Vol 1, 155
[64] Meade, 74-76
[65] Shelley, 192

defeated the Lombard Kingdom and its threat to Rome and the Pope. He defended Pope Leo from others seeking to dethrone him and was crowned the Emperor of the Holy Roman Empire by Pope Leo on Christmas Day 800.[66] The Church was beholding to Charlemagne for his protection, so they gave him this declaration, increasing his power as theirs increased, bringing a fulfilled wedding between both parties.

Charlemagne's ascension to Holy Roman Emperor gave the Pope protection and Charlemagne power. He fostered a revival of learning for the arts and prompted historians to speak of this period as one of cultural rebirth. The coronation of Charlemagne as the Holy Roman Emperor sealed his father's promise to protect the Vatican from invasion.

Charlemagne, as the recognized protector of the Church, its guardian, and benefactor, led to a new depth of unity between the Church and ruler. Charlemagne took his responsibility to the Church seriously, instituted quality control within clerical offices and monasteries, and eradicated heresy. He was a ruler of great initiative, accomplishing many achieve-ments through his actions.

Charlemagne also promoted a revival of learning in the classics and could have been appropriately defined as a forerunner of the Renaissance, although Charlemagne was not literate.

---

[66] Bainton, Vol.1, 159

## C.   The Evolution of the Papacy

1. The First Pope

Shelley describes the elevation of the Bishop of Rome to Pope:

"On June 2, 455, the Vandals entered Rome, meeting no resistance. Leo (The Bishop of Rome) met Gaiseric, leader of the Vandals, at the city gate. He was leading not soldiers but priests. When they faced each other, Leo begged for mercy; he urged the king to restrain his troops; he implored him not to burn the city; he offered money. . . the Vandals plundered the city systematically, palace by palace. Insignia, gold and silver plates, and anything that belonged to the emperor was fair game. Temple after the temple was sacked, but Rome was spared and had not been burned down. To many Romans, the Pope became a hero of someone who had negotiated for the city's safety, which led to the great power given to him, and the first person to be called the Pope was Leo."[67]

The elevation of Leo to the position of Pope cemented this designation, which has been in place for centuries and is still in place today. The reason the Pope lived in Rome and ruled from there was because of these reasons;

a. Rome was an imperial city and had much influence. The city had been powerful and influential for ages.

---

[67] Shelley, 156-157

b. The Church in Rome was the largest congregation in the world. The Roman Church bishop ascended to power.

c. The two great leaders of the Church wrote from Rome. (Peter and Paul).

d. The Roman Church sponsored the councils that decreed doctrine.

e. The Emperor gave his support to the Church. (Leo saved Rome from destruction in 455, as the Pope we already mentioned). His standing rose as the first influential Pope when this happened.

2. Changes and Reforms led by the Papacy

a. Practices introduced by the Church after receiving state sanction: Infant baptism, penance, transubstantiation, worship of Mary, praying to saints, celibacy of the priest, and the private interpretation of the Scripture by the priest and sacramental system of salvation were products of the evolution of Catholicism.

b. Infamous Popes who were corrupt: Boniface called himself the Vicar of Christ, Innocent authorized the Inquisition, Urban called for the Crusades, and Leo X opposed Luther.[68] With such a long list of other Popes spanning over a millennium, there were good and bad Popes, but all asserted the complete authority of the position.

---

[68] History World, (https://www.historyworld.net/history/-Papacy/543?section=1st8thCentury) N.D., N.A. (Accessed Nov. 8, 2024),

c. Famous Popes who strengthened the Papacy's power: Gregory the Great emphasized pastoral care, monasticism, and missions to Britain. His classic *Book of Pastoral Rules* outlined the characteristics he believed should mark a Christian minister.[69] This increasing power of the Papacy outlined for centuries to come what clergy qualifications should involve, including celibacy.

Pope Gregory the Great (540-604), sent a party of Benedictine monks to distant and barbaric England under the leadership of another Saint Augustine, who became known as Saint Augustine of Canterbury. They began a ministry in Kent, successfully established monasteries, and converted many to Christianity. Gregory pioneered the Georgian Chants.[70] He ventured into new vistas and increased the Church's power as it expanded his leadership.

Pope Gregory VII (1073-1085) stopped Simony and believed the Church was more important than the state; he humiliated King Henry of Germany. He claimed papal authority in the temporal, secular, spiritual, and ecclesiastical realms.[71] Simony was the buying and selling of Church offices and secular positions by favoritism through the Church. The practice secularized the

---

[69] Bingham, 71
[70] Shelley, 177
[71] Bingham. 89

Church and gave much to those who bribed the rulers.[72]

Each Pope seemed to have a unique emphasis. Their unified purpose was strengthening the Church's power, which meant a willingness to do so by secular rulers of the day. In a way, the Church helped precipitate civilization's trek into the Dark Ages. While countries were in constant war and ignorance of the truth in many areas (primarily the Scripture), the Church gained power and became the authority over civil powers to do what they wished.

---

[72] Simony https://www.britannica.com/topic/simony) NA, ND., (Accessed November 7, 2024)

# Chapter 6

# Medieval Monasticism and Its Influence 285-1226

Not all was gloomy in the ascendency of the Church and Pope. There were worthy movements that began with good purposes and attained some of the goals they sought to accomplish. Monasticism was one of those movements that led to these endeavors yet simultaneously restricted the learning and study of the Scripture to a select class of people apart from the populace.

Not all monastics were the same, as we shall see. Through sincerity, many renounced the cares of this world in search of a worthy goal through complete devotion to God and the Church. However, the goal led to mistakes and a deeper plunge into an ignorance of the Scripture with a solidification of the Papacy.

# A.  The Purpose of Monasticism

### 1. Total Devotion to Christ

The desire to be devoted to God was a worthy goal. The Monastic movement understood envisioned the context of the Christian quest for holiness, separation, and discipleship. Often viewed by modern-day Christians with skepticism, Monasticism continues to puzzle contemporary minds. This misunderstanding is unfortunate, for although perhaps somewhat extreme in some practices, Christian Monasticism fueled a drive to be Christ's disciples, to enter victoriously into spiritual warfare, and to flee from "friendship with the world" (James 4:4).

The movement's denial of worldly pursuits strengthened by Scripture is commendable. It was not that the Monk's renunciation of earthly possessions wasn't biblically informed, too. Renunciation imitated Christ and the disciples and followed Christ's teachings. (Matt 4:20; 6:25-33; 8:18-22; 9:21-27)[73] These sacrifices were worthy goals, but they isolated some of the most committed Church leaders and did not allow them to influence the culture withdrawing from it.

### 2. Monasticism became an Arm of the Church for Some Specific Tasks

There were multiple purposes of the Monastic movement. The monasteries were used to instruct, translate scriptures, minister to the poor, and live

---

[73] Bingham, 56-57

exemplary lives before others.[74] The isolation from the world worked well for the time and effort spent translating the Scripture and fulfilling other devoted acts.

### 3. A Specific Dedication to Christ

The self-sacrifice never called into question the Monastic's sincerity. Those who adhered to Monasticism and participated in it were totally dedicated to Christ and His call on their lives as far as they knew about Him within the context of the existing Scriptures they had.

## B. The Leading Monastics and Their Movements

1. Leading Monastic Leaders.

a. The first Monastics: The first monastics sacrificed everything. They were hermits or anchorites who retreated early to the desert of Egypt. They struggled against the forces of darkness through constant prayer, fasting, reading and reciting the Bible, and manual labor. An early leader was Anthony of Egypt.

In Syria, the hermitic life sometimes embraces extremes that are not practiced elsewhere. The Syrian ascetic, Simon the Stylite, sat atop a high column for thirty years, praying, preaching, and offering counsel to those who came to observe him. Pachomius developed a communal nature of the monastery where the monks shared

---

[74] Smith, A. "Christian Ascetics and Monks," *The History of Christianity*, (Lion Publishers: Oxford, England, 1977), 212-214.

everything. Bernard of Clairvaux wrote, "We devote ourselves to prayer not once or twice, but frequently, diligently, letting God know the longings of our hearts and letting him hear, at times, the voice of our mouth."[75] Full devotion like this highlighted those who withdrew from civilization.

b. Jerome (340-420): He began his Monastic career as a hermit in the Syrian desert but found that he could exorcise his sexual temptations only by occupying his mind with a tough intellectual discipline. He took up the study of Hebrew and found it so effective that he could venture to return to the world. He translated the Latin version of the Bible, known as the Vulgate, the first official translation from the Catholic Church.[76] It was a worthy goal to translate the Scripture. The Vulgate put the Scripture in a version many monastics could understand—the trouble came with the additional Apocrypha books, which Catholicism later accepted in its canon of Scripture.

c. Benedict (480-547): He established the first great Monastic order. He founded it to impose a life of strict discipline on all who entered the monastic life. His order lived by the Rule of a strict code of conduct, utilizing each minute of each day in purposeful activity. His monastery was in Monte Cassino, Italy.[77] This type of devotion would lead many to believe that their monastic life was

---

[75] Bingham, 55, 76
[76] Ibid, 106
[77] Shelley, 136-137

worthwhile and necessary, if not just to witness full devotion to Christ.

d. Cluny (1109-1156): He initiated a monastery in England in 910. Cluny envisioned reordering society's social fabric through Monastic, Civil, and Ecclesiastical spheres. Monasteries also served as Inns of the Middle Ages. Roland Bainton describes Cluny's way of accommodating others in his monastic order:

"Cluny had a guest house accommodating forty men and forty women and a guest master to look after the visitors. In doing so, Cluny cared for knights and noblemen who traveled. Guests were expected to contribute, but their entertainment cost was often greater than the cost of maintaining the monastery. By offering monasteries as weigh stations to knights and other nobility, Cluny's reforms aimed to eliminate feudal warfare. He was not entirely successful, but he made some impact in this regard."[78]

No movement will remain static on its own. There is always a need for reform and being fully committed to the principles of its foundation. Cluny made bold efforts to remedy the difficulties arising in the monastic movement.

e. Bernard of Clairvaux (1109-1153): The Cistercians, under their leader Bernard, were an attempt to develop a resurgence of Ascetic Monasticism that first began under Pope Gregory. The Cistercians returned to unadorned simplicity

---

[78] Bainton, Vol 1, 169-170

and would not tolerate stained-glass windows and other fancy trappings of the Church. They developed farms, grew crops, and tended flocks.

In 1115, Bernard was appointed Abbot of the monastery at Clairvaux. He subjected himself to hard labor and great privation. This appointment led to his respect and importance as a voice for the Church. He was also a marvelous preacher and a person of great moral force, as witnessed by his leadership in one of the Crusades in 1140. Bernard was a poet and a hymn writer. He justified his crusade leadership; he wrote to the Knight's Templars that killing a malefactor is not homicide but malachite (killing the bad). Clairvaux reasoned, "In the death of the pagan, the Christian is glorified because Christ is glorified."[79] This blind principle negated much of the good Bernard did in his ministry.

Clairvaux's support and call to the Crusades did not enhance his status, especially with the longevity and disappointments of the majority of the Crusades. Their very length and continuance question the wisdom of the commitment to them. Plus, there is deep hypocrisy in living a peaceful life until it involves killing one's enemies. Interestingly, he did not lead an army into battle but trusted others to do his bidding.

f. Dominic Guzman (1170-1221): Guzman led a strong movement in Spain. He began the movement sanctioned by Rome to try to bring peace to Spain between the aberrant groups in the

---

[79] Ibid, 191-194

country and France through groups such as the Canthari and the Albigenses. His leadership was influential in some ways, but the factions continued until the Reformation. He gathered a group of like-minded men and continued his work among heretics in other places

In 1220, the Dominican mission and lifestyle gained official approval; the new preaching order that we know as the Dominicans called "Mendichant," meaning "bagging," and the term "Friar," meaning "our brother," became commonplace terms to describe his group. Distinguishing friars from monks, they went forth to live among the people to preach and to teach. Teaching was a distinctive mark of this group.[80]

It would have been more helpful to the Church if there had been more friars than monks. Unfortunately, it seemed even a higher calling to be a monastic instead of a friar who lived among the common people. Explaining Church actions and the Bible would have been more helpful than reserving its teachings for the educated to study and meditate on.

g. Francis of Assi (1181-1226): Francis's order was probably the most famous because of their work among the people and not withdrawn from them. Francis was a merchant's son disillusioned with the Crusades. He renounced the world and enlisted others to follow him, taking the vow of celibacy, chastity, and poverty. The Francians, having nothing of their own in this life,

---

[80] Shelley, 229

were free to share with others freely and not be entangled with worldly attachments. His order dealt more with service to the poor and needy and modeled Christ's life of poverty and selfless service in his earthly ministry. He was so devoted to Christ in his piety that legend has it that he developed the "stigmata" to emulate the actual suffering of Christ on the cross.[81]

Francis is one of the most famous figures in Catholicism. His group did much good and served as a wonderful model, and preacher Francis became. Much of his ministry could be emulated and effectively used as a beacon for what the Christian life should look like with someone committed to having the kind of ministry Jesus modeled.

2. The Most Famous Orders Developed by the Monastics

Famous orders and their emphases:

a. Benedictines: Order

b. Cistercians, Meditation

c. Dominicans: Teaching

d. Franciscans: Service[82]

3. Other Influences of Monasticism

---

[81] Robert G. Clouse, "Francis of Assisi,' *The History of Christianity*, (Lion Publishers: Oxford, England, 1977), 271-274.

[82] These one-word descriptions are based on the author's general understanding of each order.

a. Mysticism: Monks and laypersons searched for a devoted life in the quest for the soul's transformation. In many cases, there were visions and intense asceticism. Sensations, they also believed, sometimes measured authentic spirituality. Martin Luther was influenced by this type of asceticism in Monastic life.

Several mystic leaders arose who stood out. Meister Eckhart (1260-1327) considered the goal of man to be not only a detachment from all things but the absorption of the Godhead. He was a late medieval mystic who wrote *On Solitude and the Attainment of God*, which is how we are to think of God. John Tauler (1300-1361) said that the chief end of man is to be holy, enraptured by God's love and man's love.

Monasticism and the mysticism arising from its roots developed these meditations of a life devoted to God.[83] This search in the inner life for closeness to God later appeared in Pietism and its influence, which will be discussed in later chapters.

b. Devotional works: Several devotional works were published in Monasticism. *The Imitations of Christ* was a devotional mystical book by Thomas A Kempis (1380-1471), that influenced many, and it is one of the most popular devotional classics ever written. This classic, popular among Catholics and Protestants alike, is read by many today. Non-Catholics have used A Kempis's work as

---

[83] Bainton, Vol. 1, 253

an inspirational guide leading to spiritual introspection and selfless service for Christ.[84]

c. Hymns: Bernard of Clairvaux (1090-1153) published several poetic words later translated into musical versions, such as, *Oh* the *Love of God and O' Sacred Head Now Wounded.*[85]

Chants and other songs came from the monastic influence. It was usually the closest part of music in the worship service that generally did not contain music or musical instruments.

## C. The Failures and Successes of Monasticism

### 1. Serious Devotion and Purpose

Monastery life was rigorous and hard, and there were no rewards to speak of in this type of life. The monks' daily routine had many scheduled prayer times; the first time was dawn. Their prayers demonstrated a deep dependence on God's grace, a confession of their mortality, and a healthy fear of sin. The amount of time for prayers and words in prayer was less important than the attitude. In *The Rule of Saint Benedict* (the famous guide for the Benedictine Order), he says, "We are not to imagine that our prayers shall be heard because we use any words but because the heart is pure and the spirit penitent"[86] This routine could

---

[84] Ibid
[85] John Julian, Dictionary of Hymnology (1907) https://hymnary.org/text/o_sacred_head_now_wounded, Accessed, November 7.2024)
[86] Bingham, 77-78.

not replace the needed interaction with people, ministering to them. However, they mostly stressed a pure heart and searching soul for God. Jeffery Bingham describes a typical way the monks studied Scripture:

"Monastic prayer, in its unity with Bible reading, has three phases forming a unified practice; the first phase is Lectio or reading; the second phase is meditation, or seeing the words on the page, which is insufficient. It is a repetition of Scripture leading to memorization and then purity; the final phase is an oration, or prayer is last because it is founded on the first two. Reading and meditation must lead to a response, or it is incomplete and inauthentic."[87]

This incompleteness was lacking and possibly resulted from not being associated with the world much. The influence of those who are said to be close to God was needed and is still needed today.

## 2. Retreat from the World

Reading the Bible encouraged prayer, nurtured sacred thinking, and helped the monks think correctly about God and themselves.[88] This clarity is needed to be useful in the world, which is one of the arguments against isolation.

## 3. Wasted Efforts in Many Cases

The biggest problem with Monasticism is that it did retreat from the world when Jesus asked Christians to be salt and light within it. The ideal

---

[87] Ibid, 85
[88] Ibid, 83

way of living a dedicated life in the world but not of the world is to reserve times daily for Scripture reading, meditation, and prayer, allowing those times to overshadow any worldly influence.

Monasticism had many streams, and perhaps they have not all been covered. The specific purposes, advances, and pitfalls are covered in a way that shows the good and bad of such movements.

Monasticism gave the world Martin Luther in his quest to be right with God and find salvation. It also gave us unbiblical practices given to them by the Church, such as transubstantiation and beliefs that have hurt and have not helped the influence of Christianity. A life devoted to God is a worthy goal, and the translation of Scripture was a helpful venture. How monasticism helped people personally involved in it will be told in all eternity.

# Chapter 7

# Scholasticism and its Purpose
# 1093-1517

Hand in hand with movements in the Middle Ages is Scholasticism, which intermingled with Monasticism. The scholars mostly came from the monasteries and schools. Learning restrictions to these places was the norm. Their elite learning and translation of the Scriptures made it a given that they philosophize and pontificate on these issues.

Scholasticism helped bring about an understanding of theological issues and opened up a dialogue about scriptural meaning and philosophical issues. It was not a bad move to open up a discussion of people's problems with Christianity. The debate goes on to this day. Scholars and their studies are still researching these matters. A worldwide study of the Scripture was still unavailable to the uneducated populace. An unbiased theological study was to come many centuries later. It was shameful, with only these groups studying restricted topics, which should have been unrestricted to the people and not just for the educated elite.

## A.  The Strength of Scholasticism

1. Apologists for the Church

Great thinkers arose who helped formulate doctrine and clarify beliefs.

2. These Apologists offered the Best Quality of Classical Studies.

Such a study reserved for schools of higher learning began to flourish. Great learning centers established in Europe's most popular cities fostered this study. These centered around great universities that trained priests in the classics and other philosophical works. A deeply spiritual and biblical education was missing because of a shortage of the Bible and the failure of the Church to teach its meaning.

During the Middle Ages, some eighty universities were founded, many of which have an unbroken, distinguished history to our own day; for example, Paris, Montpellier, Bologna, Padua, Oxford, Cambridge, Vienna, Prague, Leipzig, Heidelberg, Basel, Coimbra, Salamanca, Cracow, and Louvain are some of the major schools. The oldest schools operated before 1200 but were not chartered until that year or slightly later.[89] These universities were where the elite in learning came to study and pontificate. The ideas and theories

---

[89] Bainton, vol. 1, 183

shared made up the philosophy and theology of the age.

### 3. A Serious Attempt to Tackle Tough Issues

There were great scholastics at this time, although most of the populace was illiterate. The great thinkers of the age of Scholasticism were divided into two groups: the *realists* and *nominalists.* The *realists* believed in universal principles, and the *nominalists* believed in specific principles for specific people. In other words, mankind has no reality, only individual men.[90] Certainly, these ideas led to individual thinkers whose teachings were utilized or kept in check by the Church.

The *realists* supported the doctrines of the Trinity, which taught that these were universal principles and the authority of the Church. The *nominalists* questioned some of these universal principles that had application from the Scriptures. In time, the *realists* won out in their thinking and were used to supporting the Church and its authority.[91] The Church smiled on these thinkers, agreed with most of them, and sought to shun that antithetical to its teaching.

## B. Great Leaders in the Scholastic Movement

Peter Abelard and Thomas Aquinas interpreted much of the doctrine of Catholicism. Since the Church had a monopoly on education,

---

[90] Ibid, 184-185
[91] Ibid, 185-186

this reinforced Church power. Others philosophized and formed ideas that are studied to the present day.

1. Anselm (1033-1109) and the Ontological Argument for God,

Anselm argued the existence of God necessarily implies the very existence of God. Thus, by the notion of God, we mean something so great that nothing greater can be conceived; this is called the *Ontological Argument* for God's existence. It did not satisfy all theologians, but in variant form, it never ceases to attract religious thinkers. The comprehension of God proves the existence of God.[92] The built-in thinking of a higher power is the basis for this argument.

2. Thomas Aquinas (1224-1274)

He was perhaps the greatest medieval scholastic. He said we do not employ reason to test, try, or prove faith. Rather, sacred doctrine uses "human reason to make manifest some implications of its faith's message. The natural reason should assist faith." In other words, reason or rational argumentation is not the authority that ultimately renders a verdict in favor of faith.

Aquinas wrote *Summa Theologica*, which was a defense for many of the Medieval Church practices. It also employed natural reason to give evidence for doctrines and assumptions taught in the Scripture about God, the Church, and other

---

[92] Ibid, 186

teachings at that time.[93] Aquinas positioned himself as the Church's voice and is still studied and quoted today.

Aquinas examined the writings of Greek philosophers, refuted some, and incorporated some into his defense of Christianity. The result was his *Summa Theologica*, which has the whole universe in view, and in sacred doctrine, all things are treated from the standpoint of God. Aquinas made distinctions between philosophy, theology, reason, and revelation. Reason is based on visible creation, which reaches ideas that deal with faith. Revelation looks to God as He is in Himself and is superior to reason in certainty and subject matter.

Accepting Aristotle's principle – every effect has a cause, every cause has a prior cause, and so on, back to the first cause, Aquinas declared that creation traces back to the divine first cause, the Creator. This argument is called the *Cosmological Argument* for the existence of God. From a theological standpoint, Aquinas argued that man is a sinner and needs special grace from God. All who receive the benefits of Christ's work are justified, but the key, as in traditional Catholic teaching, lies in how the benefits of Christ's work are applied. Christ won grace; the Church imparts it.

Aquinas taught that Christians need the constant infusion of "cooperating grace," whereby the Christian virtues, above all, love – are stimulated in the soul. Aquinas is known as the

---

[93] Bingham, 92

greatest theologian of the Middle Ages.[94] This view of Aquinas led to the works and practices the Church prescribed to its followers. Grace is infused through the Church or withheld to those who defied it.

### 3. Peter Abelard (1079-1142)

He did much to develop the scholastic method of reasoning through his book *Sic et Non* (Yes and NO). Abelard compiled real or apparent contradictions in the writings of the Scriptures and the Church Fathers. His purpose was not to discredit the faith but to resolve the problems. When challenged, Abelard accepted the Church's authority but always sought to understand so that he might believe. In this respect, he was an architect of the scholastic method.

Abelard's affair with Heloise, the niece of Fulbert, the canon of Notre Dame Cathedral, ruined his career and credibility. She had his baby, and they retreated to the monastery and nunnery.[95] Abelard's infidelity was an issue that hurt the Church's credibility somewhat also. He had been one of its leading spokesmen and now detracted attention from his teaching by his immoral distraction.

### 4. Erasmus (1466-1536)

He rejected Luther's view of "the bondage of the will" merely because he thought the doctrine

---

[94] Shelley, 219
[95] Bainton, Vol 1, 190

was ethically useless.[96] He taught free will, a prominent feature of Catholicism. Catholics believe in salvation through good works and human effort to gain God's favor.

## C. The Problems and Challenges of Scholasticism

1. It was too involved in Minutia.

Many of the problems the scholastics tackled were far removed from the illiterate people of the time. Their arguments were exercises in futility for the most part that did not tackle the basic doctrinal issues of the Church.

2. It was High Above, Common People.

The wall of separation became very high because of the restriction of common people to the type of education the scholastics had.

3. It defended Church actions.

Scholastics did not use their learning to speak against the Church's corruption like the Reformation leaders did. They tended to look the other way at the Church's unscriptural practices.

As with many of these Dark Ages movements, there were more misunderstandings that Scholasticism did not solve. It was good to think and speak of these subjects. Yet, it would have been more helpful to understand a wider range of the common people having the Scripture and sound teaching of the Bible.

---

[96] Bingham, 108

For scholastics to be successful, they should have led to a change in the moral behavior of people during the feudal period. But as we see, the people remained in the Dark Ages. The invention of the printing press was still in the future, and the only places to get translation and ideas popularized were in areas of scholarship. So, Scholasticism was the best way to understand biblical truth through this movement.

# Chapter 8

# The Crusades and their Impact on Medieval Christianity
# 1095-1291

Possibly the greatest indication of the power of Catholicism and the Pope is seen in the Crusades. One man who claimed to be the ultimate religious authority in the world called Europe to go to the Holy Land and recapture it from the Muslim forces. Urban II's power was unbelievable in a way. So much bloodshed with widespread cruelty in battle within cities encountered by both groups of European Crusaders and the Saracen defenders was an unfortunate result.

The Pope gave added incentive, with great unbiblical offers leading to penance given to those who would go and fight to take back the Holy Land from Muslims. Whole armies were at the Pope's whelm and fought with such fierceness that could hardly be claimed for the forces that fought under the banner of the cross. The battle's fierceness and the lives lost led to difficulty in understanding doing all this in the name of Christ. Such were the times, however, and the world was shattered by such battles and fighting in the land where the Prince of Peace lived, taught, died, and rose from the grave to bring peace. Yet such peace was unseen in such horrendous fighting, cruelty, and death.

## A. The Purpose of the Crusades

Understanding the purpose of the Crusades is crucial to looking at their mark on history. Their purpose was to take back the Holy Land and offer safe passages to pilgrims. Many shrines built there were in danger, and the Church did not want to see the Holy Land in the hands of the Muslims. The early Muslim rulers had guaranteed Christians the right to visit the holy places without molestation. However, restrictions got worse, and many Christians were killed, imprisoned, and abused, increasing the tension there. Pope Urban II called for a crusade to remove the Holy Land from these occurrences.[97] The plea for peace for those Christians in the Holy Land led to all-out war.

A unified "Christian Europe" as a Coalition was one of the positive results of the crusades.

---

[97] Albert Neuman, *A Manual of Church History Volume 1*, (Ancient and Medieval Church History), Judson Press: Valley Forge, 1932), 457-458

Europe joined together in following the Pope's urging in an unparalleled display of solidarity.

The Crusades were also an opportunity to take the danger away from the Eastern Church, representing a branch of Christianity in the outpost of the Muslim Middle East. If they fell, all of the Middle East would be Moslem.

## B. Different Crusades and their Specific Purposes

1st Crusade 1095

Called by Urban- The First C"rusade was primarily French. The Council of Clermont had been attended only by the French, among whom there were four groups of participants. Urban's hope seemed to have been that the holy places should be delivered from the Turks and then turned over to the Eastern Empire, but the Crusaders were not so interested and were soon at odds with the Eastern Empire and each other.[98] The Eastern Church did not get much relief from the impending dangers they faced from foreign invaders.

2nd Crusade 1147

Led by Bernard of Clairvaux, who called for the crusade to take back the places of pilgrimage. His motive was personal piety, but those who went to the Holy Land turned it into greedy gain. It achieved absolutely nothing to speak of. All the places and passages gained in the First Crusade were lost.

---

[98] Bainton, Vol 1, 179

3rd Crusade 1187

The 3rd Crusade, noted for its famous leaders of the Crusades, led to an expansion of the nation's fighting to take the Holy Land back. Richard, Philip, and Fredrick fought. They went to the Holy Land and led their respective armies, giving them greater notoriety than the other Crusades. It is probably the most renowned Crusade because of these principal players. Shelley describes how:

"In 1187, Saladin, the Sultan of Egypt and Syria, brought fresh and vigorous leadership to Muslims when Jerusalem fell to the infidels. Christians, with some reluctance, responded to the cry of the Third Crusade in 1189. The leaders were three of the most famous medieval kings, Fredrick Barbarossa of Germany, Richard the Lion-Hearted of England, and Philip Augustus of France. Fredrick drowned in Asia Minor, and after many quarrels with Richard, Philip returned home. Saladin and Richard remained the chief protagonists. To keep the Muslims united, Saladin proclaimed a jihad, or Holy War, against Christians. Richard and Saladin finally agreed to a three-year truce and free access to Jerusalem for Christian pilgrims."[99]

These events, though, did not spell the end of hostilities in the Holy Land.

The Sack of Zara by Crusaders 1202:

This unfortunate event happened during the Third Crusade. Zara was a Christian city in the Eastern Empire. The crusaders plundered the town

---

[99] Shelley, 208

for gain and killed many innocent lives. Pope Innocent III threatened to excommunicate all who participated, but none were brought to accountability, making this Crusade a sham.[100] The incident remains one of the truly low points in the Crusade era.

4th Crusade and Other Lesser-Known Crusades (1200-1291)

The Fourth Crusade (1202-1204) led to miserable fracture and division resulting from an insult. The Eastern Church refused to acknowledge the Roman Church's authority, and Pope Leo IX excommunicated the patriarch of Constantinople, the head of the Eastern Church. The Eastern leader of the Church excommunicated the Pope's delegation.

This division solidified the schism between the two Churches, which began with the two Churches due to language differences and the use of icons. In 778, the Roman Church forbade this practice, which continued in the Greek Church, as well as territorial disputes and various beliefs like celibacy in clerical office.[101] These differences and distance led to an unrepairable schism that spoiled one of the Crusades' goals of protecting the Eastern Church and its adherents.

The Latin Empire in Constantinople lasted until 1261, but the ancient city never fully recovered. The conquest widened the schism

---

[100] Ibid, 209
[101] Bingham, 91

between the Greek and Latin Churches and hastened the city's fall in 1453 to the Turks. The protection in Constantinople as a goal for the Crusades was never fully realized.[102] The Holy Land went back and forth over the possession of the land, leading most armies never to get there to defend or take it back.

## C. Movements Involved, and as a Result of the Crusades

### 1. Templer Knights

These were knights who, for the most part, fought in the Crusades. Surviving and coming home, they were more loyal to the Pope they had fought for than to the civil ruler and country they returned to. Bainton describes them in more detail:

"They were an obstruction to the civil leaders of their day because their allegiance was only to the Pope, and they had no civil allegiance. The knights were wealthy and armed, and the leading warriors led the charge for the Pope in retaking the Holy Land in the Crusades. However, with the crusades over, they defied the authority of the civil rulers, and Philip of France trumped up charges of blasphemy against them. Their entire order in France suffered arrest overnight. Fifty-nine Templers were burned in Paris in 1314 as a sign of their defiance. Their allegiance illustrated their sincerity to the cause of the Holy War."[103]

---

[102] Shelley, 209
[103] Bainton, Vol 1, 229-230

The Knight's resistance to Civil authority illustrates a clash between the secular and the spiritual, even leading to a physical war.

2. Trade Routes to the East

The travel to the East brought a new curiosity for Eastern staples and items. This route led to gain and increased exploration.[104] Economic gains were a boon of the crusades.

3. A Unified Europe in Defending the Holy Land

The crusades featured an entire European effort to defend and fight together, taking some of the emphasis off of feudalism that had plagued Europe in the Dark Ages.[105] Instead of civil war, a united front was brought against the Muslim leaders.

The bloodshed and sacrifice of many lives overshadowed the good accomplished through the Crusades. The energy exerted in one century continued through several centuries. It seemed the energy ran out after so many crusades and so many lives sacrificed based on false promises and lives lost. What was gained did not seem to be as valuable with the lives lost and witness to the world as being unchristian.

If this is what Christianity was, it significantly harmed any witness attempted in the name of Christ. One wonders how these atrocities could be linked to the Christian faith and regarded as

---

[104] Newman Vol. 1, 462
[105] Ibid, 462-463

needful to preserve the Christian places and witness to the world. If one looks at the whole spectrum of the History of Christianity, the Crusades and the Spanish Inquisition stand out like sore thumbs as terrible witnesses and lie about what the Christian message is and how the Crusades were used as an excuse for rejecting such a distorted message of Christianity.

# Chapter 9

# The Condition of Medieval Christianity 800-1450

Back on the home front, the move from authentic Christianity to superstition and ignorance was prevalent all over. The illiteracy, lack of education, and learning only for the elite and clergy were plunging Europe into darkness. The Dark Ages were a time of darkness for the message of Christ and the understanding of its role in culture and people's lives. The beliefs and practices adopted and mandated by Catholicism were far removed from the teachings and ministry of Christ, which resulted in the expansion of the Christian movement in the First Century.

Eyes turned from biblical truth, leaving people in spiritual darkness. The Bible was not available and in print. Many of the illiterate people relied on the Church for truth. Yet, they did not find enlightenment, only darkness. This darkness pervaded the landscape for what the Church had under their sway. The light was still centuries away as the Church moved further away from the true message of Christ and His teachings. The souls left in darkness indicated how the Church had moved far away from the spiritual power that infused the gospel's message with authority that came from heaven. The study of Christian History would be empty without seeing these teachings codified in the Church. These teachings did not rescue people from the darkness of sin but led them astray from biblical truth.

## A. The Period is Dominated by Superstition and Biblical Ignorance

1. No Scripture Read

The Church owned the Bible and would not allow the laity to have it. There was no common translation. Most of the population was illiterate, and the priests could only translate the Scripture into Latin.

2. Major Aberrations Arose to Christianity

a. Celibacy: Priests remained celibate, but there were abuses and embarrassments to the Church for those who could not control their passions.

b. Treasury of Merits: Saints stored up good works and were prayed to so they might go to God for the petitioner based on their good works. Direct mediation of Christ to the Father, forbidden in this thinking, was replaced falsely by the need for a human intermediary and contributed to this perversion. I Timothy 2:5 refers to Jesus as our only mediator, and we can come to Him directly without needing an intermediary.

c. Papal authority (infallibility): The Pope's belief in being completely right in all matters of faith and practice led to other abuses. He could decree, excommunicate, and command armies. He was more powerful than Scripture and ensured salvation was only through Rome.

D. Transubstantiation: The teaching is that bread and wine become Christ's body and blood in their communion. The laity was only allowed bread. This forbiddance, in effect, offered up Christ for eating at every mass.

e. Indulgences: A release from Purgatory purchased from the Church taught the departed soul could be set free. The practice was prevalent in Luther's time but used before this time.[106]

## B.  Conflicts of Church and State

1. The Investiture Controversy-

The clash between state and religion came with this memorable event leading to a historic confrontation that Bainton reports:

"The Church won its victory over authority with the civil rulers. When Hildebrand, who took the name Pope Gregory VII, was elected Pope, he demanded the cessation of lay investiture, which

---

[106] The above list is a general understanding of the unique teachings of Catholicism as encountered by myself. It is a general definition I give based on my decades of dealing with the subject.

met with stout resistance on the part of the rulers in Germany because abbots and bishops had a dual role. The rulers could choose their Church officials. However, his view won as Gregory VII tried to return the Church to a religious base instead of being a puppet of the civil rulers."[107]

The worldliness of the Church had led to such controversies and, in this case, pitted the Church against the State, which had an original agreement.

2. Henry IV and Gregory VII

Henry IV of Germany appointed the Archbishop of Milan. Pope Gregory accused him of Simony and Lay Investiture. He excommunicated Henry and placed Germany under interdiction. (Interdiction means the whole country is under excommunication). Henry came to the Pope's villa (1077) and waited in the snow for three days to see him. He repented for exercising power over the Pope, being absolved by him, with the interdiction removed. But the power of the Papacy over civil rulers had reached its zenith.[108]

3. Becket and Henry

The battle between Church and state came to a boiling point in England. Thomas A Becket was appointed Archbishop of Canterbury by King Henry II in England. Henry wanted to control the Church through him, but Becket turned against the King and excommunicated him. Henry had Becket

---

[107] Bainton, Vol. 1, 173
[108] Ibid, 175-176

assassinated, but it stained Church-State relations in England. The date for this conflict was 1170.[109] Henry tried to fight the Church and repented of assassinating his friend, thus bowing to the Church's power.

### 4. The Great Schism

Rulers began to jockey for a Pope who came from their country. This division resulted in seventy years of the Papacy moving to Avignon, France, under the control of the French rulers. The "Babylonian Captivity of the Church," as it is so-called, ended in 1377. Bainton enlightens on the controversy between Popes:

"Pope Gregory XI perceived that the Papacy should be cut loose from France if other countries did not renounce obedience to the Holy See. Gregory XI returned to Rome, but his cardinals refused to accompany him and elected another Pope who stayed in Avignon and took the title Clement VII. He and his successors at Avignon are not recognized by the Roman Catholic Church today, and that is why, at the time of the Reformation, another Pope bore the title Clement VII. There were, however, two Popes and two sets of cardinals during this time, and they were not fully terminated until 1459."[110]

Now, the big question was which Pope was the right one. The Church could have only one Pope.

---

[109] Latourette, Vol.1, 481
[110] Bainton, Vol, 1, 234

Martin Luther was fond of reminding the Church leaders of the fallacy of Papal Infallibility since there was a claim laid to the throne of Peter by two groups of competing parties. The way to resolve the claim of Papal Infallibility was through a movement called Conciliarism, which would mean that different councils of the Church would decide on Church policy to be ratified by the Pope. This policy has continued until this day.[111] The controversy led to an even greater power of the Papacy. The Pope's selection would be a total inside job without outward interference.

## C. Evolving Doctrine and Power of the Universal Church

### 1. All of Europe is Catholic

At times, threats to the power of the Universal Church arose from the Albigenses and the Waldenses (followers of (Peter Waldo). They did not recognize the authority of the Roman Church nor believed that its sacraments had power over those who participated in them. In response to these groups, the Catholic Church began strong persecution and, in many places, annihilated pockets of resistance from these groups.[112] The anti-Christian response to such groups proved the hypocrisy of the Church in dealing with dissidents. They persecuted and killed them, leading many to expose any spiritual power or authority they had with God.

---

[111] Ibid, 234-235
[112] Ibid, 213

2. Protection and Power of the Pope

The Holy Roman Empire and Civil rulers were used at the whelm of the Pope in the Crusades with promises of material gain to solidify the Pope's power and protect him from all adversaries.[113] This power did not come from God but relied on civil authorities for their validity and nchristian actions.

3. Popes controlling the Destinies of Rulers.

Conflicts ensued with civil authorities. In 1296, Pope Boniface VIII threatened ex-communication against any layman who extracted taxes from the clergy without the Pope's permission. In England, controversy existed between Becket and Henry II and King John, who was required to pay tribute to the Pope against his will.[114] Special protection and hypocrisy were the characteristics of the Church during this time of strengthening its might. The Church stood against Henry II for his murder of Beckett and demanded penance and his brought under the Church's prominence.

Political corruption and immorality in the Vatican reached unbelievable heights under Roderigo Borgia, who ruled as Alexander VI (1431-1503). He was grossly immoral and obsessed with a passion for providing wealth and power for his children.[115] Such hypocrisy and immorality made the Church a laughingstock to the world. It made

---

[113] Newman, Vol. 1, 459
[114] Bainton, Vol.1, 227, 216
[115] Shelley, 241

it easy to demand reform that allowed such a person to be exalted as Pope and practice immorality.

These heavy-handed exercises by the Church became a harsh reality:

a. Excommunication means consigning someone to Hell and removing them from the Church: Thomas Becket did this with Henry II.[116] The Church's power over secular rulers was amazing and something they were not afraid to exercise and bring these rulers to their knees.

b. Interdiction means placing a whole country under a ban from church rights and the sacraments: Gregory VII exercised this power over Henry and the Country of Germany.[117] It was certainly unbiblical and unbelievable that a nation brought to its knees came begging for forgiveness from the Pope.

c. Anti-Popes: It was ridiculous to have several Popes all at once. There were three Popes at one time for 72 years. This confusion happened (as mentioned) when Louis established the Papacy at Avignon, France. The Italians established another Pope when each excommunicated the other. A third Pope was elected, but no one stepped

---

[116] "*Thomas A Becket*," *History of England*, https://www.historic-uk.com/HistoryUK/HistoryofEngland/Thomas-Becket/, NA, ND, (Accessed November 9, 2024)

[117] Justo L. Gonzalez, *The Story of Christianity*, Vol. 1, (San Francisco: Harper and Rowe, 1984), 283.

down. This controversy lasted 72 years.[118] At times, it was difficult to determine who was excommunicating who. It was a real low point for the Church.

Sinful inventions and lust for power were culprits in seeing Christianity stoop to its lowest level since the Christian movement started. These practices led to a deeper distance from New Testament Christianity. The need for truth, relief from ignorance, and the tyranny of the Church empowered by civil rulers was apparent. Out of desperation, the cry came for the truth, which some were brave enough to stand for against such glaring faults of the Church. By this time, the Church had reached such a realm of power that they stomped out any dissension to call for the truth over the norm's ignorance.

One can look back on this period as the after-effects resulting from the division from biblical truth. It was a time of desperation until a great movement would rescue so many souls being led into darkness and remaining there. Some would stand up against the Church's tyranny, studied in future chapters as those who found truth and wanted to spread it but were shut down and erased by the corrupt Church of the time.

---

[118] Ibid, 340

# Chapter 10

# Forerunners of the Reformation 1174-1498

The morning stars of the Reformation highlighted in this chapter illustrate the need for change. These individuals saw the corruption and false teaching of Catholicism and stood against it while standing for the truth. Those who stepped forward were dissenters who had never been a part of the universal religious system and those within it who called for reform and removal of unbiblical practices.

Many of these groups and individuals just started ministering and practicing New Testament truth. Those who risked the fallout from being a voice of dissent and a return to New Testament practice were exposed. They would come under the iron hand of the Church with the backing of civil power and yielding unchallenged power so that any dissent was difficult. However, their courage was unyielding when they either renewed New Testament practices or spoke directly against the unbiblical and immoral behavior of some Popes and religious leaders who defended the Church regardless of their errors and practices.

# A. What Abuses and Ideas the Leaders Spoke About

### 1. Transubstantiation

They saw this against scripture, the finished work of Christ, and the laws of nature.

### 2. Papal Authority

They believed the Pope had a level of authority that he had falsely assumed and should be given only to Christ, as revealed in the Scripture.

### 3. Scriptural Accessibility

The question of where authority came from for belief and practice was simple since most scholars translated the Scripture and saw it contrary to the Church's practice.

### 4. Purgatory and Indulgences

Purgatory was unfounded in the Scripture, and a person's eternal destiny became set at death and not changed through indulgences or any other means.[119]

# B. Revolutionary leaders in the Pre-Reformation

1. Saint Patrick and his Missionary Spirit (386-459)

Patrick was a missionary to Ireland who preached the gospel and baptized many converts by immersion. He preached all over Ireland, and many turned from paganism to Christianity. He did not acknowledge the authority of the Pope and used baptism by immersion for those who became Christians, as evidenced by the many baptismal pools found in Ireland.

Patrick was a Briton who was kidnapped and put into slavery in Ireland. Although released, he returned to Britain later and developed compassion for the Irish people. He was reared a Christian and felt called to return to Ireland and preach the gospel to them.

Patrick refused to acknowledge the Church's authority in Rome and baptized by immersion converts who came to him in the churches established. W.A. Criswell's (Former Pastor of First Baptist Church of Dallas) understanding of Patrick's practice came through personal research of his family history. His ancestor's last name was originally "Christ well." His history means that

---

[119] (Based on the author's understanding of the abuses by the Papacy during the Middle Ages and the Pre-Reformation period).

many of Criswell's ancestors experienced baptism in a well, and through immersion, they declared their faith in Christ and took "Christ well" as their last name. The middle T dropped through many centuries, along with h, and left his recent ancestors the name "Criswell." Dr. Criswell traced his ancestors back in Irish history, their conversion to Christianity, and subsequent baptism afterward. Criswell's study of his family is very helpful in understanding Patrick's ministry practice.[120]

Although there is a significant gap between the forerunners of the Reformation and Patrick, his classification in this list is because most of his messages related to the doctrine of salvation by faith and his baptisms by immersion revealed in the many baptismal pools of that area. They indicate his allegiance to the New Testament method of baptism by immersion.[121] Believer's baptism seemed to be the order of the day when he led many to Christ, and his followers continued his practice.

2. Peter Waldo (1140-1218)

He was a rich merchant in Lyon, France. Shortly after marriage to a rich nobleman's daughter, he vowed to live a life of self-denial and poverty. Hearing a wandering troubadour singing

---

[120] W.A. Criswell, W.A. Criswell Sermon Library, Dallas, TX, Sam Hull administrator: St. Patrick was a Baptist Preacher, 1958 (accessed December 27, 2015), http://www.wacriswell.com/sermons/1958/st-patrick-was-a-baptist-preacher/
[121] Bainton, Vol, 1, 143

the virtues of the monastic life, he reappeared and provided an adequate income for his wife, placing his two daughters in a cloister and giving the rest of his estate to the poor. He launched a mission to the poor and enlisted two priests to translate portions of the Bible into French. After memorizing long passages, Waldo began to teach common folk to imitate Christ by practicing voluntary poverty. He sent his followers out two-by-two in the apostolic pattern. They identified themselves as poor in spirit and were known as the "Waldenses."

Waldo's unauthorized preaching soon met stiff opposition from the Archbishop of Lyon, who ordered him to stop. He refused by quoting Acts 5:29, "We must obey God rather than men." The Waldenses wanted to purify the Church by a return to the simple life of the apostles. This teaching meant the surrender of worldly power. The Papacy had not renounced the sacraments or its exclusive priesthood nor admitted that faith in God might be something other than the mandates of Rome.

The Waldenses were so clearly a "back to the Bible" movement that, over the years, many evangelical Christians tried to present them-selves as Reformers before the Reformation. Shelley believed that the Waldensian's call to return to the Bible sounded like Luther's or Calvin's. Still, their view of salvation, penance, and poverty lacks the clear note of God's grace that sounded so powerfully in the Reformation.[122] It is difficult to understand why the Church would persecute such

---

[122] Shelley, 225-227

a movement, but the Waldenses did not see any hope for the Church to institute reform. They faced the iron teeth of the Church because of their courage and refusal to relent to the iron hand of the Church.

3. John Wycliffe (1324-1384)

He was an English reformer who rejected many ideas of Catholicism. His followers were called "Lollards." They memorized the Scripture and preached what they memorized.

Wycliffe was also the first to question Papal authority granted the Papal schism that occurred for seventy years. He also found the ethical deportment of the Popes whose lives were a glaring contradiction to those of the apostles, were not successors of the apostles nor the true Church of the elect but manifestly reprobate. Wycliffe believed the priest could not change the bread and wine into the body and blood of Christ by transubstantiation because there is no transubstantiation. Scripture simply verified this understanding. He began to interpret the Bible in contradiction to the wishes of the Church at that time.[123] Wycliff's refusal to substitute error for truth led to the Church seeking him and his follower's destruction. The fact that they were not next door to the Vatican helped allude their immediate capture and attempts to silence them.

Wycliffe's denial of transubstantiation gave his enemies their opportunity, and he was

---

[123] Bainton, Vol. 1, 237-238

effectively silenced at Oxford by the Bishop of Canterbury in 1382. Wycliffe gained enough support that the Church authorities had the good sense not to move against him. The Reformer died in 1384. On learning of his death, the Papacy dug up his bones and scattered his ashes in the Thames River, which flows to the Atlantic Ocean. However, it turned into something positive and symbolized his teachings, starting in England and flowing to the whole world.[124] What meant to be an embarrassment was now a testimony of Wycliffe's biblical teaching going into the world. Such schemes would not stop the truth from standing against the false teachings of the Church.

4. John Huss (1369-1415)

He was a priest from modern-day Czechoslovakia who favored reading the Scripture, baptism by immersion, and freedom from the Universal Church. He began to preach and explained the Bible verse by verse. The crowds who came to hear him at his local parish Church could not fit into the Church building.

Huss was influenced by John Wycliffe's writings after his ordination and was appointed rector and preacher at Bethlehem Chapel. Huss began to study Scripture and had serious doubts about the lifestyle of many of his day's immoral and decadent popes. The chapel where he spoke increased by massive numbers as he went through

---

[124] Newman, Vol. 1, 606-607

the Bible in his preaching and teaching the Scripture.

Huss was summoned to the Council of Constance in 1414 to present his views to Church authorities. Upon arrival, he found himself a victim of an inquisition. He was asked to recant heresies, which he always stoutly disclaimed. For Huss, the truth was supreme. He exclaimed, "I have said I would not, for a chapel full of gold, recede from the truth." For eight months, he lay in prison, his letters during the last month rank as great Christian literature. Finally, he was condemned by the council after being promised safe passage. Shelley details Huss's actions in going to his death:

"On July 6, 1415, the day of his burning came; on the way to the place of execution, he passed through a churchyard and saw a bonfire of his books. He laughed and told bystanders not to believe the lies circulated about him. He knelt and prayed. His last words were, "God is my witness that the evidence against me is false. I have never taught or preached except to win men, if possible, from their sins. In the truth of the gospel I have written, taught, preached; today I will gladly die."[125]

What Huss had taught, he now sealed it with his blood.

Huss's primary contribution was the move to a more biblically oriented congregation, which caused him trouble. He questioned Rome's

---

[125] Shelley, 249-251

authority and believed in giving the Lord's Supper in communion to the laity.[126] These practices in Huss's Church stood as an open practice against the Church that wanted to suppress it and silence his actions.

5. Girolamo Savonarola (1452-1498)

Called the "Morning Star of Reformation," he preached from the Bible against the power of the Papacy. Savonarola did not use the liturgy but trusted the Lord for messages from the Scriptures. He spoke out against Rome's hypocrisy and the Popes' corruption. Savonarola's parish Church was located in Florence, very close to Rome, thereby putting him in range of the wrath of the Church. He was tortured, tried for heresy, and when he would not repent, was burned at the stake.[127] Savonarola stood firm against the hypocrisy and immorality of the Church. He would not bend and, through it all, was remembered for his strong stand against what he believed was evil and falsely represented in the Church.

## C. Progress and Disappointment in Confronting Church Corruption

1. The Pre-Reformers set the stage for the Reformation

The grievances ignored, the corruption of the Church, and the contradiction with scripture made it only a matter of time before revolution occurred

---

[126] Bainton Vol, 1, 239-240
[127] Gonzalez 353-356

and gave the world freedom of religious expression.

2. People suffered and died for convictions contrary to Catholic Doctrine.

Many martyrs killed during this time of opposing Catholicism are recorded in history. Incidences such as the Crusades and the Spanish Inquisition are blights in the History of the Church. The corrupt nature of the Papacy during this time, with several Popes fathering illegitimate children or leading armies to war, also was a stain upon the Church.[128]

The Spanish Inquisition has been one of the biggest blights of Catholicism in its History. It proved the evil motives and ignorance of the State Church relationship. Jews rounded up in Spain suffered imprisonment, and many suffered martyrdom if they did not accept the Church's teaching to be Christian in the perverted doctrine they used to massacre the Jews.

The Church even tried people loyal to the Papacy, such as Joan of Arc in 1431. Civil power was the most important factor for the Church instead of truth and Scripture.[129] Since her martyrdom, Joan has been respected and exalted

---

[128] Borgia Popes,
https://kids.britannica.com/students/article/Borgia-Family/273298#:~:text=Through%20Cesare's%20efforts%20the%20Papal,during%20a%20battle%20in%20Spain.&text=Lucrezia%20Borgia%20(1480%E2%80%931519),died%20on%20Jun., (Accessed November 11, 2024), N.A., N.D,,
[129] Latourette Vol. 1, 645-646

to sainthood, so the initial ignorance and hostility toward her are gone. The ignorance of the Church in burning her at the stake is seen now as cruel and heartless.

## 3. The Response of the Church

The Church was strong enough to extinguish these voices of reform temporarily. Yet the brave reformers set the stage for the Reformation and the power of the state leaders to get behind voices of change, leading to a massive overhaul of the Universal Church.

At the end of the 15th century, the world was desperate for true Christianity, which had disappeared from the Church in many quarters. Dissenters could see what the Church did to those who dared to speak against their immorality and false teaching.

The truth could not be dismissed despite the dark canvas of the Church's false teaching, which needed a light to shine on its errors and behavior. The question was, where would this fearless voice come from? Would it come from inside the Church or those dissenters on the outside looking in? Something had to happen, and the enlightenment in many areas seeking to rise as the sun to the darkness could not have come at a more needful time. Who would rise on the horizon to bring biblical truth back?

# Chapter 11

# Luther and the Protestant Reformation 1517-1555

Lighting struck across the horizon in the person of Martin Luther, a monk in Germany. History records that the Reformation was the dividing line between truth and error in the Universal Church. It was an attempt to bring people back to the truth of God's Word and what it said, particularly about salvation and the authority of Scripture.

Luther's struggle, in a way, represented all of humanity. There was the desire to know God and be right with Him. The salvation offered in Christ obscured by the attempt of the Church to be the only authority over people's lives was a stark reality. So far, they had been successful in keeping dissent in check, at times severely using the state to strike down people's search for the truth through brute force. It was dangerous to oppose the Church no matter how far it had strayed from the real truth of the Bible. Yet, Luther courageously stood against the hypocrisy and corruption that had become the Church's trademark and needed to be opposed and corrected. Luther had no plan to establish a new Church, but the after-effects of his opposition would put him and all who loved the truth of God's Word on the outside looking in.

# A. Luther's Life, Preparation, and Conversion

1. Childhood and Youth of Martin Luther (1483-1546)

Martin Luther was raised in a family of means. His father hoped that he would pursue a legal profession, but he went in another direction and became a priest. Luther greatly disappointed his father's desires when he entered the priesthood. His protection from being struck by lightning in a rainstorm caused him to promise St. Anne he would be a monk.[130] His father greatly opposed his entering the priesthood but could not stop him. Once in the monastery and taking the vow, he struggled with his sin nature, seeking to be pure in his relationship with God.[131] His struggle was real in spirit and afflicted him even physically.

2. The Priesthood

After Luther became a monk, he encountered corruption in the Universal Church during his pilgrimage to Rome. He continued a desperate

---

[130] Roland Bainton, *Here I Stand, A life of Martin Luther* (Abingdon: Nashville), 26-27, 34.
[131] Ibid, 41-42

struggle to be accepted by God and gain forgiveness for his sins. His devotion to fasting, praying, and observing self-imposed rules led him to come up empty in his desire to find God.[132] Outward habits and strict searching brought no rest to his soul.

### 3. Salvation/Justification

Here is a portion of Luther's testimony that Bingham records:

"As a monk, I led an irreproachable life. Nevertheless, I felt that I was a sinner before God. My conscience was restless, and I could not depend on God being propitiated by my satisfaction. . . Then, finally, God had mercy on me. I began to understand that the righteousness of God is that gift of God by which a righteous man lives, namely by faith – the righteousness of God is revealed in the gospel – the merciful God justifies us by faith, as it is written: 'The just shall live by faith.' Now I felt as though I had been reborn altogether and had entered Paradise."[133]

With Luther's rebirth spiritually came hope and promise for the future of Christianity and its teachings.

---

[132] Philip Schaff, *History of the Christian Church* Vol. VIII, (Grand Rapids, MI: Eerdmans),118-119.
[133] Bingham, 115

# B.  Abuses Luther Challenged

## 1. Indulgences

Luther attacked the sale of indulgences because they a. diminished the free, gracious gift of salvation; b. did not evoke true contrition or repentance; c. did not produce the Christian virtue of love, and d. were ultimately the opposite of Christian virtues of mercy and compassion.[134] It was unthinkable that money could buy a soul out of purgatory. Luther had to fight against its practice out of a strong obligation to the truth and the desire to expose false teaching.

The sale of indulgences, introduced during the Crusades, remained a favored source of papal income. In exchange for a meritorious work-frequently, a contribution to a worthy cause or a pilgrimage to a shrine church offered this sinner redemption from his acts of penance by drawing on its "treasury of merits." This consisted of the grace accumulated by Christ's sacrifice on the cross and the meritorious deeds of the saints.

All too often, the zealous preachers of indulgences made them appear to be a sort of magic…Sorrow for sin was completely and conveniently overlooked. This practice troubled Luther, as Shelley details:

"Luther criticized the selling of indulgences through Dominican John Tetzel, specifically, who preached throughout much of Germany on behalf of a Papal fundraising campaign to complete the

---

[134] Ibid, 113

construction of Saint Peter's Basilica in Rome. Luther was aroused by Tetzel's method of selling indulgences in Germany. The thought of buying salvation was repulsive to him. Luther challenged this abuse by nailing his 95 theses to the Church door at Wittenberg. He challenged the abuses of the Church, particularly the selling of indulgences, and the Protestant Reformation began on October 31, 1517."[135]

Now, the great contest started with the teachings of Christ and the Bible, battling the authority of the Church's unbiblical practice.

2. Papal Authority over Biblical Authority

Luther replaced Papal authority with Biblical authority, particularly regarding salvation. In his pamphlet, *The Babylonian Captivity of the Church*, Luther questioned the Church's and the Pope's authority. He found no biblical justification for several key Church teachings, and the movement began to hinge on his leadership.

Luther also made clear justification by faith, reshaping the doctrine of the Church. He argued that Rome's sacramental system held Christians "captive." He attacked the Papacy for depriving the individual Christian the freedom to approach God directly by faith, without the mediation of priests. He set forth his views of the sacraments.[136] He did not see any saving value in the sacraments. It was

---

135 Shelley, 258-259
136 Schaff, Vol, VIII, 213-214

used as a work to gain forgiveness of sin and eternal life.

Luther said a sacrament had to be instituted by Christ and be exclusively Christian to be valid. Of these tests, Luther could find no justification for five of the Roman Catholic sacraments.[137] This introspection by Luther created quite a firestorm that led to conflict and public accounting of the Church.

3. Works Salvation as Opposed to Justification by Faith

The showdown with the Catholic Church allowed Luther to declare his beliefs without timidity, as Bainton indicates in his narrative:

"Luther began translating the Scriptures at Wartberg Castle and defined the Justification by Faith and The Priesthood of Believers. These factors became the foundational truth of the Reformation. The Pope summoned him to the Diet of Worms and asked him to answer for his writing in April 1521. At the hearing, he acknowledged his authorship but refused to repudiate them. Fredrick of Saxony protected him, and the Holy Roman Emperor Charles V tolerated this protection."[138]

Luther was fortunate to be in Germany, a country willing to shelter him from physical danger. He declared his conscience with the protection of the German princes.

---

[137] Shelley, 259
[138] Bainton, *Here I Stand*, 90-96

Luther did not deny his teaching of justification by faith at the Diet of Worms when he debated John Eck, a Roman Catholic scholar. In his sermon "Two Kinds of Righteousness," Luther explained that any righteousness coming forth from believers has its source in the righteousness given to them in Christ. There is no intrinsic human righteousness unless one first receives an "alien" external righteousness from God through Christ.[139] Jesus' death on the cross could only provide this righteousness as an atonement for our sin. One must trust in His sacrificial death for our sin to have this internal righteousness implanted within us. Then, through the power of the Holy Spirit, we bring forth works of righteousness that prove our salvation.

## C. Luther's Contribution and Effect on the History of Christianity

1. A Courageous Stand against the Most Powerful Institution on Earth

Luther was branded a heretic by the Church, an outlaw by the Pope, and a hero by his fellow countrymen. His beliefs became the basis for the Lutheran Church. At the Diet of Worms, he said, "My conscience is captive to the Word of God; I can do no other God help me." Luther's associate, Philip Melanchthon, formulated the Augsburg Confession in 1530, and in 1555, the Peace of Augsburg established Lutheranism as the official religion of

---

[139] Bingham, 116

Germany.[140] Luther's life, spared through the civil magistrate's protection, furthered Protestantism's cause.

Charles V, the Holy Roman Emperor, declared Luther a criminal, but he was protected by Fredrick the Wise, the Prince of Saxony, who kidnapped him and brought him to Wartburg Castle. During this time, he translated Galatians and emerged to see the social order of Germany change as they stripped off the bonds of Catholicism and became a Protestant nation.[141] The translation of the New Testament greatly helped the cause of Protestantism in Germany, with the common man now able to read the Bible in their language.

2. Luther broke the Stranglehold of the Church on the Conscience.

Luther's great testimony at Worms that his "conscience was captive to the Word of God" was proven to be a reality in what the Reformation did. It replaced Papal authority with God's word as the basis of our faith and practice.[142] This authority of the Bible trumped the Church's authority on the most important doctrine of salvation, determining the destination of our eternal soul.

3. Luther Ushered in the Reformation

a. Luther encouraged others: The breakthrough for religious freedom led to a break with Rome, the establishment of the Reformed

---

140 Ibid, 323-325
141 Shelley, 260
142 Latourette Vol. 2, 719-721

faith, and the Anabaptist movement. Thomas Munster's Peasant Revolt in Germany was an attempt at social upheaval on the back of the Reformation.[143] Critics of the Reformation used the rebellion to point out what happens when the Bible and its teachings are given to the populace. However, bad rebellions such as this needed toleration to get to the truth of the Bible and practice its truths.

b. The Reformation led to Protestant State Churches: Luther retained belief in the Universal Church, infant sprinkling, consubstantiation, and government-sponsored religion. He also did not stand up for groups like Ana-Baptists to dissent.[144] These groups felt Luther did not go far enough in the Reformation and wanted to be biblical in their beliefs.

c. Confessional statements: The Augsburg Confession in 1530 gave way to others who confessed a biblical faith instead of putting trust in tradition over the Bible.[145] They gave an understanding based on the number of Confessions of Faith that arose in the 16th and 17th centuries relating to understanding biblical truths, not traditional Catholicism.

---

[143] Dan Nelson, Early Baptists: A Comparative Study of the Anabaptists and English Baptist Movements, Faithful Life Publishers: Fort Myers, FL), 2018, 47.

[144] Ibid

[145] John Leith, editor, Creeds of the Church: A Reader in Christian Doctrine from the Bible to the Present, The Revised Edition, John Knox Press: Atlanta, 63-106, 1963.

The dye was cast, and the world would be better for Luther's stand. Although Luther stood alone initially against Rome, the civil power supporting the Church now supported him and his right to establish the truth. That truth gave people the Bible in their language because of his firm stand and opposition to the unbiblical practices of the Church.

Now, the loosened rock that released an avalanche would release a storm of others standing for truth and freeing people to be free from the shackles of false teaching in the Church that demanded their obedience. Certainly, the Bible's openness to the populace was a key factor, for it supported the truth and rebuked the false teachings and hypocrisy of the Church. Now, others would come forth and herald the truth of God's Word. Even they would disagree on matters, but now salvation was nigh even at people's hearts and not far away in Rome with certain representations and control of local parishes. Now, truth brought people the open-ness of the Bible, taught by leaders who would support Luther's opposition to the Church and establish those churches that would stand for the truth.

# Chapter 12

# Calvin and the Reformed Movement 1536-1564

John Calvin was the next figure to step forward and articulate the truth of the Reformed movement. Calvin's life and ministry are interesting studies. His attempt to continually and descriptively explain the contents of Scripture helped many understand the Reformation and its thrust.

Calvin's teachings have survived to the present day, and his exegesis of Scripture set the next stage of the Reformation. Clarity and explanation marked what he taught. Calvin's greatest contribution was probably to those who went all over Europe and into America with his teaching. They were inspired by it and used by God to rescue nations with new freedom and independence from Catholicism. The same institution had kept so many from the truth of Scripture and the freedom to believe and practice what the Bible taught.

# A. Calvin's Life and Stronghold in Geneva

### 1. History and Conversion of Calvin

John Calvin (1509-1564) grew up in France and had become severely disenchanted with the Roman Catholic leadership. He believed the clergy was misleading and uncaring despite thinking he needed to be redeemed. We are unsure of the precise date of his conversion, but we know it occurred sometime between 1532 and 1534.[146] Whenever it was, he became a true believer in Christ, which tremendously impacted his life and ministry. Bingham gives a good sketch of Calvin when he says:

"Calvin's background was impressive. This background evidenced itself in his ministry. He trained in the law and desired to study the classics, but his interest in theology superseded everything. Calvin wrote the first edition of his doctrinal masterpiece, *The Institutes of Christian Religion*, in French in 1536 at the age of 27. Later editions appeared in Latin. The work, revised twenty-six times, attempted to understand the Scripture that the laity could now read."[147]

---

[146] Latourette Vol.2 752
[147] Bingham, 118

Calvin's work explained truths and doctrines that were central to biblical under-standing.

### 2. Exodus to Geneva, Switzerland

Calvin narrowly escaped with his life from France. His friend Guillaume Farel (1498-1565), the leader of the Reformation in Geneva, encouraged him to come to Geneva. He was encouraged to move there, where the Reformation was already underway. What Luther had done for the Protestant cause in Germany, Calvin did for the same cause in Switzerland. His first period. in Geneva ended in 1538 when the city's government evicted him. In the eyes of the local magistrates, he and Farel had placed too much authority in the Church and not enough in the city council.[148] His overriding the council's actions with scripture brought him to clash with them, ending in a showdown.

### 3. The Development of the Stronghold of Church and State in Geneva.

Calvin had wanted to bring moral and doctrinal reform to Geneva but left because of conflict with the city leaders. He was in Strasbourg, where he remained until he returned by invitation to Geneva in September of 1541. This time, authority over religious issues lay in the hands of both the Church and City Council. Calvin continued to minister in Geneva until his death on May 27, 1564. This theocratic type of government lent

---

[148] Ibid

freedom for him to teach and be the major influence in the city.

Calvin believed in a strong state-sponsored religion and did not tolerate others who disagreed, such as the Baptists. Calvin still retained infant baptism, the Universal Church, and opened the door to Hyper-Calvinism, which is a fatalistic view of the pre-determinism of God. Extreme Calvinism denies man's free will and becomes a detriment to evangelism.[149]

## B. The Theology of Calvinism and God's Sovereignty

1. Institutes of the Christian Religion.

Calvin formulated what has been called "Reformed Theology." His teachings were also used by Ulrich Zwingli, who persecuted the Anabaptists in Zurich, Switzerland. Zwingli died in battle, and Calvin became the leader of the Reformed movement in Switzerland. His teachings and writings established Calvinism as a dominant theology in Christian History.[150] The protection in Geneva gave him freedom to extend his influence and teaching. Luther and other leaders (especially the Anabaptists) did not enjoy this freedom to instruct.

*The Institutes of Christian Religion* was the clearest, most logical, and readable exposition of Protestant doctrine that the Reformation Age produced. It gave its youthful author European

---

[149] Schaff Vol. 8, *The Swiss Reformation* 83-84, 184-185
[150] Shelley, 277

fame overnight. Twenty years later, it was a much larger work, but its interpretation of Christian truth remains essentially the same. This interpretation attempted to bring the main thoughts and doctrine of Scripture to people. It was a good understanding of salvation and its benefits in one's life.

*The Institutes* formulated Calvinism and centered on the irresistible grace of God. Calvin defined salvation as a gift; man is totally depraved with a sin nature, and God's grace is everlastingly justifying the sinner who is unworthy to save himself. This later view is known to many as eternal security.[151]

Calvin moved to the other side of salvation, seeing it as a gift of God in His sovereignty. This view was the opposite of Catholicism's teaching for centuries.

2. Specific points:

Calvinism is incorporated into the acrostic TULIP. Adherence to this system determines how strong a Calvinist you are. TULIP means:

a. T-otal Depravity: Man is born with a sin nature that makes him dead because of his sin. He can only be awakened at salvation by God's spirit.

b. U-nconditional Election: God individually predetermines what will happen to a person concerning their salvation experience or lack

---

[151] Keith v Mathison, Ligonier Ministries, Oct 16, 2018, https://www.ligonier.org/learn/articles/john-calvin-and-doctrine-irresistible-grace, (Accessed Nov. 14, 2024),

thereof. When we trust Christ, we confirm God's election in our life.

c. L-imited Atonement: Christ died for those who would believe in Him. He did not die for those who will not trust him as Savior.

d. I- irresistible grace: We are saved totally by God's grace and His work without any human effort of our own.

e. P-erseverance of the Saints: All true saints of God persevere to the end and are kept eternally secure by God for all eternity.[152]

Through these letters, one gets a comprehensive understanding of Calvinistic Theology.

## C. Lasting Contributions of the Reformed Movement

1. Salvation is All of God.

Even regenerated Christians can never offer their works to God as a basis for justification. They always depend on Christ's righteousness because even the "good works" of the Godly deserve condemnation when examined in detail.[153] God takes the initiative in Christ as a sacrifice for our sins. Our faith and trust in His provision as a free gift is a work of God based on what he has done on our behalf.

---

[152] John T. McNeill, The History and Character of Calvinism, Oxford University Press: Oxford, England), 264-265.
[153] Bingham, 119

2. Calvin articulated the Doctrine of the Reformation.

Calvin did not believe the people of his generation understood the Bible. He felt that he needed to teach systematically through the Scripture to help people understand its contents and thereby be changed through it. In doing this, he was articulating the major doctrines of the Reformation.[154] Understanding the Bible was a worthy goal. Calvin's systematic teaching added even greater understanding to the doctrines of Scripture.

The Treaty of Westphalia in 1648 provided a religious settlement. Calvinism was accorded the same status as Lutheranism and Catholicism; its territorial status stabilized according to the prevailing conditions of January 1, 1624. The Treaty precluded interference from the Church of Rome in religious matters in Germany.[155] The wars that started over which denomination would be protected and extended in a certain country were violent and shameful.

3. There was a Strong Sense of Purpose wherever Calvinists went through leaders and movements.

a. John Knox (1505-1571) and Scotland: John Knox was a follower of Calvinism and trained in Geneva, went to Scotland, and established the

---

[154] Biographical Presentation of John Calvin, by Steve Lawson at The Shepherd's Conference, Grace Community Church, April 2012
[155] Bainton, Vol. 2, 63

Reformed Church as the State Church of Scotland. He stood against Mary, Queen of Scots, who tried to return the nation of Scotland to Catholicism. His influence was so strong, Mary said. "To have feared the prayers of John Knox more than any armies massed against her."[156] Knox was a steadfast champion who prevented Catholicism from returning to Scotland.

b. The Puritan Movement in England: Many Puritan leaders arose after the great Civil War, leading England to a more biblical understanding of the Scriptures in worship and practice. Leaders such as Richard Baxter, John Owen, Christopher Love, Thomas Manton, and Thomas Watson greatly influenced the direction of England towards the Reformed Doctrine. *Pilgrim's Progress* by John Bunyan has strong Calvinistic overtones.[157] These leaders afforded Calvinism a steady expansion and major influence in England.

c. The Puritan Emphasis in America: The Reformed movement was influenced particularly in New England through the transplanted Puritans. Great theologians such as Jonathan Edwards and many Puritan pastors like Cotton Mather articulated the five points of Calvinism and made New England a stronghold for Puritanism.[158] This emphasis carried over to the New World and was

---

[156] Newman, Vol. 2, 240-242
[157] Peter Lewis, *The Genius of Puritanism*, (Soli Deo Gloria Publications: Morgan, PA), 11-18.
[158] Newman, Vol.2, 287-291

instrumental in founding and sustaining a religious influence in America.

As Calvinism spread through the Western world, a revival of teaching and understanding of the Bible continued. The effect of Calvin's understanding and straightforward direction to accept and live by its truth was carried across the ocean to America.

Calvinistic teachings exposed affected governments and countries, as with the English Civil War. The attention given to the ruler's acceptance of its tenets or opposition to them went back to the Catholic model. Victories won, and trends established through Calvin's effort to teach the contents of God's Word became central to his ministry. Calvinism allowed others to understand its truth and left a mark on the world through his tenacity to bring the truth of God's Word to nations and people.

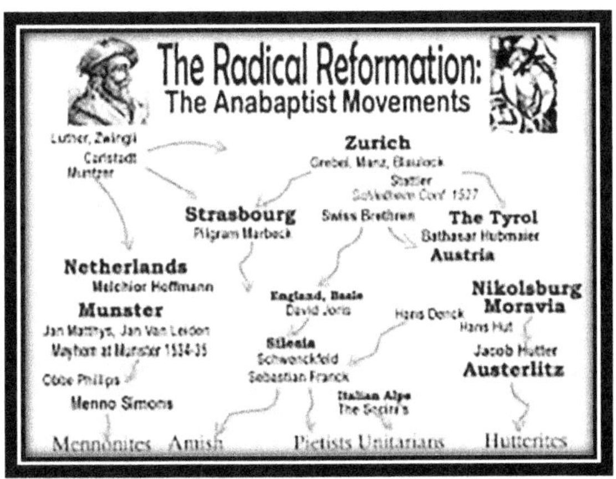



# Chapter 13

# The Radical Reformation and its Place in Christianity 1525-1550

The Reformation brought the freedom to examine the Bible in a way not studied before. Guttenberg's invention of the printing press did much to put the Bible in the hands of the common man. Luther and Erasmus's translations of the New Testament led to many other Bible translations that opened the door for many different renditions of the Bible, which would be prevalent in the 16th century.

What the Bible taught was now in full view, and the teachings of Scripture were evident to all who would study and read it. Now, many understood the practices of Catholicism as they discovered the Reformed Movement. Some practices were still alive in the Reformed Movement. The Anabaptists' strong belief in believers' baptism by immersion (eventually) and the fact that there was no State Church put them in conflict with Ulrich Zwingli in Switzerland and other Reformed leaders. They felt that the only Church in the Bible was the local assembly of baptized believers. They felt infant baptism led people to a false sense of salvation since it initiated them into the State Church and, in some places, made citizens out of them, as in Zurich.

The Anabaptists challenged Luther and Ulrich Zwingli in Switzerland on the issues they felt were important that the Reformation had ignored. They were descendants of others who had believed in such truths and were free from Catholicism. They suffered persecution because of it, just as the Anabaptists did by Protestants and Catholics.

## A.  History of the Anabaptist Movement

### 1. The Need for a Believers Church

Baptist History goes back to the time of Christ when certain groups with an affinity for Baptist principles operated outside the framework of the Universal Church. Such groups were the Donatists, Albigenses, Waldenses, Petro-Brussians, Arnoldists, and certain individuals who advocated Baptist principles. Baptists did not start with the Protestant Reformation. They were only defined as a group and began using the name Baptist during the Reformation. They believed the Bible was their source of practice, unlike Luther and Calvin, who advocated a mixture of tradition and the Bible.

Baptist leaders believed only in the Church as a local assembly. They rejected the idea of a State Church that included everyone in a family regardless of their capability of faith. Individuals who had not come to personal faith in Christ counted as Christians being citizens, contradictory to what the Bible taught.[159]

In Zurich, Switzerland, the Anabaptist Movement began. As they met in a group, George Blaurock, a former priest, stepped over to Conrad Grebel and asked him for baptism in the apostolic fashion – upon confession of personal faith in Jesus Christ. Grebel baptized him on the spot, and Blaurock baptized the others. Thus, Anabaptism, another important expression of the Protestant Reformation, was born.[160] However, most of the Protestant leaders opposed the movement. Ulrich Zwingli would become its archenemy, trying to drive it out of Switzerland.

On March 7, 1526, the Zurich City Council decided that anyone found re-baptized or teaching such doctrine would be tried for heresy, and some were eventually martyred for this practice. They thought, "If heretics want water, let them have it." They also mandated that all newborns be baptized under their law. The Anabaptists resisted their mandates. Within a year, on January 5, 1527, Felix Manz became the first Ana-Baptist martyr. The Zurich authorities drowned him in the Limmat river,

---

[159] Henry C. Vedder, *A Short History of the Baptists* (: The American Baptist Publication Society, Philadelphia, 1907),.24-28, 130.
[160] Newman, Vol. 2, 170-173

which flows through the city. Within four years, the Radical Reformation in and around Zurich was practically eradicated, but the Anabaptist movement in other places began to grow.[161]

These sacrifices, as Manz and others made, opened the door of dissent to Protestant leaders like Zwingli, who would try to erase the truth of the Bible with traditional teaching and control by the State Religion.

The distinctive statement of the Anabaptist movement is *The Schleitheim Confession*, written in 1527, which is a strong statement about individual conscience and religious liberty.[162] Although this confession did not completely state Anabaptist doctrine, it did show how the local Church should function free from the state Church that was persecuting it. Michael Satler, the soon-to-be martyred leader, was the primary author of the Confession.

2. Following the Biblical Teaching of Baptism

The Anabaptists eventually saw baptism only by immersion and said it must be for believers, so they refused to sprinkle their infants. This belief got them in trouble with civil authorities in Germany and Switzerland.[163] These authorities persecuted them, tried to get them to recant, drove them out

---

[161] Shelley, 268-269

[162] Weaver, Daniel. J, Becoming Anabaptist: The Origin and Significance of Sixteenth-Century Anabaptism. 2nd ed. Scottdale, PA: Herald Press, 1987, 61.

[163] William Estep, The Anabaptist Story. Grand Rapids: Eerdmans, 1975

of the country, and eventually killed their leaders who stood up for the truth of the biblical teachings of the Church and baptism.

### 3. No Solidified Movement

The Anabaptist movement became known as the "Radical Reformation" because it advocated the local Church and a complete break with the civil government's right to regulate religion. They felt Luther and Calvin did not go far enough in the Reformation; they essentially saw them cleaning out the Catholic Church concept. Anabaptists did not advocate house cleaning but advocated an entirely new order. They are spiritual ancestors of modern-day Baptists and stood against the tide of public opinion for truth instead of accommodation to error.[164]

Some Baptists would not agree that the Anabaptists were related to modern Baptists, but all one has to do is look at their teaching and practice and discover a certain similarity.

Because Baptists had the unfortunate distinction of being persecuted by Catholics and Protestants, their leaders did not live long. The movement that came from Anabaptism was not as powerful as the Lutheranism and Calvinism Movements for this reason.[165] A common understanding is that there is a scarcity of Anabaptist works that survive and a minority of

---

[164] Nelson, Dan, *Early Baptists*, 23

[165] A common understanding is that there is a scarcity of Anabaptist works that survive and a minority of people who know about them outside of modern Baptists..

people who know about them outside modern Baptists.

## B. Leaders and Movements from Anabaptists

1. Conrad Grebel was the group's first leader in Zurich, Switzerland. He led the group along with Felix Manz.

2. George Blaurock was the first person baptized by Grebel. He became a strong leader exiled from Zurich after being beaten when Felix Manz suffered martyrdom.

3. Felix Manz was the First martyr for Anabaptism on January 5, 1527, when he was punished by drowning for his stand on believer's baptism.

4. Hans Denck was a leader of the Anabaptist with Michael Sattler in Germany.

5. Menno Simons founded the Mennonites and was the leader and founder of many churches in Holland. His movement prospered with less government resistance, as in Switzerland, Germany, and Austria. Simons was a former priest who left to enter the Anabaptist movement. Churches eventually saw less persecution of the movement he led. As the movement's leader, Simons formulated Church practice, which denoted strict discipline and autonomy. His ministry was primarily in Holland. Simons was strong on Church discipline and accountability.

6. Balthasar Hubmaier was the spokesman for the movement. A former Catholic priest, he was

also arrested and burned at the stake on March 10, 1528, in Austria after being captured by Francis Ferdinand Archduke in Austria.

7. Michael Sattler was a former priest who became a spokesman for the Anabaptist movement in Germany. He opposed government regulation of religion. Sattler also led people to disobey the government in an unjust war against the Turks. He was burned at the stake for his leadership and refusal to cooperate with a primarily Catholic government.[166]

## C.  Basic Tenets and Legacy of Anabaptists

1. A Believers Church and Individual Accountability.

Anabaptists believed babies should not experience baptism and that every person baptized should be a believer who had accepted Christ personally. They believed saving faith in Christ, and this alone was a requirement for Church membership. The Church, therefore, was a local body of believers and not an institution or invisible as the Catholics and Protestants had taught.[166] The Anabaptists had the New Testament teaching on their side and took what it taught literally. They did not keep traditions for peace in the country. They did not accept practices like infant baptism, no

---

[166] A Complete and thorough description of these leaders and their biographies are covered completely in my book Early Baptists: A Comparative Study of the Anabaptist and English Movements.

matter who stood for it and how popular It might be.

2. The Biblical view of the Ordinances was symbolic to the Anabaptists.

Anabaptists believed baptism was a presentation or a declaration of what had already happened in one's life, and the Lord's Supper remembered the sacrifice of Christ for their sin. Because of their view of baptism, Anabaptists refused to allow the baptism of babies. Their view of non-violence in many cases also led to the persecution of its leaders, primarily by Zwingli and leaders of the Reformed movement in Switzerland, as they turned civil authorities against them.[167] The ordinances had no saving power in themselves. Any carryover from Catholicism that was for salvation and not because of salvation was opposed even though they suffered persecution and death.

3. Religious Liberty

The Anabaptists did not believe the civil government should control religion. Their bloody history of being persecuted and martyred for their faith is an example of government regulation of religion that has gone astray.[168] God never ordained the government to decide religious matters and mandate a certain practice.

The Anabaptists laid the groundwork for the Baptist movement in England and America. Other groups had an affinity with them, but the Baptists

---

167 Nelson, *Early Baptists*, 140-141
168 Ibid, 194-195

believed they correctly interpreted the Scripture, especially regarding believer's baptism and the local Church.

The Anabaptists took up the mantle of dissenters before them, which had many doctrinal similarities. Others would follow the Baptist movement and prosper in areas where persecution was less prevalent than in Switzerland, Germany, and Austria. The trailblazing movement that brought about a willingness to live totally by the Scripture continues today. Despite early persecution, the Anabaptists returned to the Scriptures and its message, resulting in many Baptists Churches in the following centuries.

# Chapter 14

# The Counter-Reformation and its Response to Protestantism 1540-1555

Catholicism was shaken to its very core with the Protestant Reformation. The great movement demanded a response from what was happening in Europe and eventually the New World. The Jesuit movement did rescue Catholicism from the ash heap, but what were they rescuing them toward? The Council of Trent sent a message to Catholics and the rest of the world about how they would respond to the Reformation movement. This Protestant movement would not result in returning to the fold.

The Catholic Church's response would seal their fate for the next new centuries by dealing with what had rocked the world. It was an opportunity to start afresh and reform from within. But despite this great opportunity, it seemed to be more of the same. The practices added through the centuries with no renouncement didn't result in joining these movements in search of the truth of Scripture. The world changing around them did not diminish these beliefs and led to them double-downing on what they had practiced for centuries.

## A.   History of the Jesuit Movement

1. Conversion and Direction of Ignatius Loyola (1491-1556)

Loyola's tenacity and drive resulted in a movement to establish Catholicism in places it had never been before. The movement he founded and sanctioned by the Church resulted in gains for the Church from the losses of the Reformation.

Loyola was a former Spanish soldier who had a deeply moving religious experience in a hospital while recovering from battle. He devoted himself to becoming a soldier of Jesus and the Catholic Church. Shelley shares how the Jesuits began under Loyola's leadership:

Loyola, a young Spanish nobleman, was injured while fighting the invading French at Pamplona and defending his homeland. He professed conversion to a disciplined life in service of Catholicism. He reduced his rebirth at Manresa to a plan of spiritual discipline, a military manual for stormtroopers at the service of the Pope. The result was that the Jesuits, the Society of Jesus, were the greatest spiritual force in Catholicism's campaign to recapture the domain that had ceased with Protestantism.[169]

The Jesuits were a militant group when it came to extending the influence of Catholicism and getting into countries and areas that had no connection with the Church.

2. The Purpose of the Jesuits

Loyola gathered a strong group around him to extend the influence of Catholicism. By militant discipline, Loyola recruited followers whose goal was to preserve and restore the glory of the Catholic Church. His order received official endorsement from the Pope, and he began to send missionaries all over the world, particularly to the Orient.[170] They went everywhere with a central purpose and direction. They would try to expand the Church's influence and go beyond the traditional countries that previously supported Catholicism but were now Protestant.

In Rome, the Catholic Church became more militant and approved Ignatius Loyola's new "Society of Jesus." These daring soldiers of Christ promised the Pope they would go wherever he might send them, whether to the Turks, Lutherans, or others, be they infidel or faithful.[171] They had a supreme allegiance to the Pope. The movement would try to take back what Catholicism had lost in the Reformation.

---

[169] Shelley, 289
[170] Ibid, 294
[171] Ibid, 292

3. The Exploits of the Jesuits

Francis Xavier was another leader who expanded Catholicism around the world. Xavier's missionary efforts extended to China and Japan.[172] The Jesuits established Catholicism worldwide on other continents, such as South America. They were willing to educate the Native Americans in Catholicism and endured much hardship through the rigid discipline that Loyola had mandated. Essentially, the Jesuit movement saved Catholicism from oblivion.[173] The Church got up from its down position because they were willing to make sacrifices and go anywhere. Their emphasis on education also was a welcome respite from holding back information from people.

## B. The Councils of Trent and its Response to Reformed Doctrine

1. Anathemas were given on:

a. Justification by Faith: It refuted salvation by grace through faith, and salvation by works was affirmed.

b. Scriptural Authority: The Bible was not the final authority for faith and practice. The traditional teaching of the Church was their authority.

c. Protestantism and their Church: They did not recognize any Protestant Churches as legitimate.

---

[172] Ibid,295
[173] John Donnely. "The Jesuits," *The History of Christianity*, 420.

d. Transubstantiation: They still affirmed that the body and blood of Christ transformed into elements during communion.

e. Those who denied Sacramental Salvation were anathematized: Salvation was not by faith but through partaking of the sacraments.[174]

Standing up for these practices, regardless of their non-biblical origins, was a disappointment in many cases regarding a rapidly changing world, with old world orders quickly evolving.

2. There was a Clear Division between Protestantism.

The Council continued to hold to salvation by works, the sacramental system, and Papal authority while vowing to regain the territory lost to Protestants. This division and the Church's response through The Council of Trent is important because it officially clarifies and puts the Church's position of salvation by works in writing. Although the Jesuits set out to regain the world for Catholicism, Trent was a major backward step.[175] Instead of trying to find agreement with Protestantism, they magnified the very reason Protestantism opposed them and double-downed

---

[174] Word Explain, Contemplative Theology, Contemplating Roman Catholicism, Edited and translated by J. Waterworth (Dolman: London), 1848.

https://www.wordexplain.com/Anathemas_and_the_Council _of_Trent.html, (Accessed Nov. 15, 2024),
[175] Shelley, 295-296

on their acceptance despite the opposition around them.

Pope Paul took action on a few items, but most significant was his response to calling a general council. The council called in 1545 seemed noble, but the general declarations did not come from the council until 1555.[176] Ten years to develop statements was unbelievable, especially with an understanding that they wouldn't change much with their beliefs and practices.

3. No Real Change in the Church

The Council of Trent is the official document of the Catholic Church. Many individual Catholics may believe differently, but Trent is the "law of the land" that the Church has operated under since this council was convened and officially gave a response to the Reformation, which was, "We are not going to change." Instead, they reinforced their efforts to spread Catholicism everywhere.

From start to finish, the Council of Trent reflected the new militant stance of Rome. Everything the Protestant Reformation stood for vigorously, and one could almost say violently, was rejected at Trent. The Protestant Reformers emphasized justification by faith alone; the council insisted that Christian people must perform good works lest they become lazy and indifferent.[177] Each pronouncement brought opposition and a certainty that the Protestant movement, once and

---

[176] Ibid, 292
[177] Ibid, 295

for all, would be sealed from any return to the Church because of Catholicism's will not to change or even accept Protestant teaching.

Luther, Calvin, and Grebel stressed salvation by grace alone, and the Council emphasized grace in human cooperation with God to avoid, in Loyola's terms, "the poison that destroys freedom." The Protestants taught the religious authority of Scripture alone, and the council insisted on the supreme teaching of the office of the Roman Church, Popes, and Bishops as the essential interpreters of the Bible.[178] They would add to the interpretation of Scripture only as it flowed through the funnel of the Church.

# C. Catholicism Then and Today

1. Consistent themes

a. Papal infallibility: The Pope is the head of the Church on earth.

b. Works salvation: Salvation is by works, not faith in Christ.

c. Tradition over Biblical authority: Tradition trumps what the Bible says.

2. Comparisons- Catholics hold some doctrines in common with Protestants.

a. The Trinity: Both believe God is revealed through the three persons of the Father, Son, and the Holy Spirit.

---

[178] Ibid

b. The Virgin Birth: Both believe in the virgin birth of Christ, but Catholicism exalts Mary to the form of Godhood and co-redemptrix.

c. Biblical morality: Both groups support a biblical view of Scripture. Evangelical Churches are more accountable to Scripture because they know what it says.[179]

3. Changes from the Reformation

a. No more militarism in the Catholic Church: Catholicism no longer had the civil authority to enforce its teachings everywhere it went. The Pope drew a line of demarcation for exploration in the New World between Spain and Brazil. Columbus did not enforce conformity to religion, but Cortez and Pizzaro did in their explorations and conquering of the peoples in Mexico and South America.

This attempt to convert the natives to Catholicism led to "Christo-pagan" religions.[180] These aberrations came from the refusal of the Church to believe in biblical practices and producing a biblically illiterate position of converts to Catholicism.

Junipero Serra (1713-1784) established missions later in present-day California, bringing

---

[179] A Common Summarization of basic beliefs held solely by Catholicism and those they have in common with non-Catholics

[180] William, Madsen, *Christo-Paganism. A Study of Mexican Religious Syncretism*. Tulane University. Middle American Research Institute. (Preprint from Publication 19, New Orleans, 1957), 105-180.

Catholicism to the world and California.[181] The sacrifice of men like Serra still made Catholicism a force reckoned with because men like him were willing to go anywhere with the dissemination of their faith.

b. Tolerant attitude toward Protestants: The Catholics believe Protestants are "fallen brethren" and would gladly welcome them back into the fold. However, they now recognize that the split is inevitable after 500 years and seek a better relationship with them.

c. Working with Bible-believing Churches: Bible-believing Churches need to be cautious because of the Catholic view of salvation and other superstitious beliefs related to the sacraments, praying to saints, and many traditional teachings that are not scriptural. However, many Bible-believing Christians do cooperate with Catholicism in matters such as the pro-life movement, the influence of Christianity in government, the biblical view of marriage and the family, and other issues that do not relate to doctrine.[182] Discernment is essential in seeing the greater good in cooperating with Catholics on moral matters that could make a difference in the culture.

---

[181] Rita Sporleder, https://ewtn.co.uk/chpop-the-amazing-life-of-saint-junipero-serra-apostle-of-california-first-saint-to-be-canonized-on-u-s-soil/, June 30, 2024, (Accessed November, 16, 2024).
[182] General knowledge of Catholic cooperation with other Christian groups

The Protestant Reformation is one of the greatest events in history. The return to Biblical Christianity, as we know it, helped poise Christianity to impact the world in a truthful way that we have experienced up until the present day. Yet, Catholicism stands in the way of many of the Protestant Reformation's great truths.

Catholicism has so many problems with contradicting Scripture today, where there still is much biblical illiteracy. The Counter-Reformation could have been a time of renouncing what was false and not fighting to support it. The Council of Trent is still in effect today, and there has been no other council to address, as they would call, "their fallen brethren." Because of this great omission, the Council of Trent and Catholic's response to Bible-believing Christians is insufficient and a failure to bring any unity with believers all over the world.

People can find true salvation for Catholics, but it is usually despite the main teachings of the Church. Salvation can only be found in an open Bible, not contradicting traditions. For this reason, many are religiously lost today despite their entrenchment in religious groups that do not preach the gospel. God honors His Word and not artificial practices that contradict it.

# Chapter 15

# The English Reformation: Henry the Eighth to the Glorious Revolution (1534-1688)

Much of our heritage today in Christian belief and practice has come from the native country of the early settlers in America. England has produced a sad state of religious events, great truths, and influential individuals. Much history has been made, and there is a great void in understanding the History of Christianity if we do not study England's Religious History.

Religious liberty and great truths of Scripture were evolving into much of what we believe and practice as Christians. Many individuals and rulers have been in conflict or supportive of movements and events that have shaped the Christian landscape of the world. What we experience in churches has much of its roots in English Christianity and the individuals God used to shape it. These happenings are expansive in many areas, with confessions, civil wars, rulers favorable or unfavorable to the truth, and movements that have survived tremendously.

# A. Religious History in the 16th Century

1. Henry VIII (1491-1537) as Head of the Church of England

The Church of England was established through Henry VIII's dissatisfaction with the Pope, who would not give him a divorce. The structure was very much like Catholicism, with ritualistic worship, sacraments, hierarchy of priests, and many other similarities. Henry divorced his wife and went through several. Edward, his son, followed him and died suddenly at 18.

2. William Tyndale (1494–1536)

He was one of the most famous English Bible translators in English History. He worked on this task at a time when it was illegal to translate the Bible because of Catholicism's hold on the Bible and the desire not to have it disseminated to the populace. Henry desired to stop Tyndale, and he had to flee from England to continue his translation and its shipping back to England.

Tyndale's desire for an English translation was a vision he had to combat biblical ignorance in his home country. Tyndale is best known for working tirelessly to get the English Bible into the hands of the common people. The Church of England strongly opposed him as they considered the English Bible a threat to their power. This threat involved the Church's keeping people ignorant of the Bible's teachings and message.

One of the Church's bishops argued with Tyndale, saying it would be better for the people to have the Pope's law than God's. To this comment, Tyndale famously replied, "I defy the Pope and his laws! If God spares my life, a plowboy shall know more of the Scriptures in a few years than you do."[183]

Henry did not allow freedom for any groups outside of the Church he was establishing. He ordered Tyndale captured and the destruction of his famous Bible translation.

Tyndale's capture and demise demonstrated Henry's fierce hostility to groups seeking religious freedom in his new Church or with such views. Tyndale was eventually strangled and burned at the stake as a heretic. Yet, his work carried on. Some estimated that more than 75% of the 1611 translation of the King James Bible was Tyndale's work. This translation made it into the hands of many plow boys.[184]

Tyndale's last words before being strangled and burned at the stake in 1536 were, 'Oh Lord, open the King of England's eyes.' The martyr's prayers were answered in 1539 when King Henry VIII allowed the Bible in every parish Church in

---

[183] Steve Brandon, "Enjoying His Grace and Extending His Glory,"
https://enjoyinghisgrace.wordpress.com/2016/01/27/the-plow-boy/, January 27, 2016, (Accessed November 12, 2024)
[184] Ibid

England. The King James Bible, published in 1611, also was an answered prayer since it featured most of the text taken directly from Tyndale's translation.[185]

## 3. Queen Mary (Bloody Mary)

The closeness to Catholicism of the Church of England was realized when Mary (1516-1558) became the Queen and quickly switched the country back to Catholicism in little time while martyring many dissenters and scholars. She banned Bibles in Churches and imprisoned many leaders of the new Church. Mary had the backing of the Church in Rome to bring England back into the fold. She burned dissenters in a place called Smithfield, which saw many people martyred there. She had a short reign and died after four years on the throne.

## 4 Elizabeth's Mediation of the Church

Elizabeth (1533-1603) sought a compromise to let the Church of England be Protestant, but it was not determinative in its change. The Puritan movement was born during this period, expressing dissatisfaction with the slowness of the reform in the Church.

---

[185]Mary Wimberley, Tyndale's Will to 'One Thing' Resulted in English Bible
https://www.samford.edu/news/2009/Tyndales-Will-to-One-Thing-Resulted-in-English-Bible#:~:text=Tyndale's%20last%20words%20before%20being,Bible%20was%20published%20in%201611, October, 30, 2009, (Accessed November 20, 2024).

Elizabeth wanted to quell the religious storm. She seemed to turn a deaf ear to the Puritan's criticism. Great discoveries and feats accomplished great things during this time. The defeat of the Spanish Armada in 1578 thwarted England from becoming Catholic again.[186]

5. Separatists from the Church

Dissenters arose but were swallowed up by the state's power to control religious affairs. Small groups began to emerge and offer an alternative to the shallow religious environment of the state Church. From these groups, the Baptist movement began. John Smyth's congregation at Gainsborough and John Robinson's at Scooby started as Separatist groups. Symth and Thomas Helweys were leaders of a Baptist congregation who fled to Holland with their congregations. Helweys eventually returned, leading to the first Baptist Church building on English soil. They joined several other groups, such as the Brownists, led by Robert Browne, and the Ancient Church, with Francis Johnson as dissenters to the Church of England.

The dissenters realized the State Church concept in England would never work and was responsible for the false security of many that it was a Christian country. They could not abide by much of the vestiges of Catholicism in the Church of England.

---

[186] All the history of the English Crown under Henry and his predecessors are common facts and history derived from public knowledge of these episodes

While these groups separated from the Church of England, the Puritan movement started in the Church, hoping to purify it and remove vestiges of Catholicism from the State Church.

## B. James and Charles' Conflict with Puritanism

James I (1566-1625) followed Elizabeth and asserted the "divine right of kings." This belief means the Almighty gave the King's law to outrank everyone else.[187] The Puritans and Separatists desired that he rid the Church of Catholic influence. They wanted the Bible in the hands of the people. The Puritans wanted images and liturgy removed from services and the preaching of the Word to be primary. They also deplored *The Book of Common* Prayer, introduced by William Laud, Archbishop of Canterbury.[188] Laud was harsh in his enforcement of the use of the book and strict in his demanding churches to conform to it. Shelley reveals:

"James was harsh in his attempts to save the Church of England from too much Puritan influence. On only one point did King James I consent to the demands of the Puritans. He was willing to have a new translation of the Scripture produced. From this decision came what we call the King James Version of the Bible. On nothing else of significance, would the King be held to the Puritans? The ceremonies, the Prayer Book, and

---

[187] JSTOR Daily, "Making Sense of the Divine Right of Kings" https://daily.jstor.org/making-sense-of-the-divine-right-of-kings/, NA, ND, (Accessed November 7, 2024).
[188] Bainton Vol. 2, 79

the bishops of the Church of England were going to stay."[189]

The King James Version seemed to be a bargaining chip in which he tried to satisfy the Puritan's demands by authorizing the Bible version.

Some early Bibles were translations leading up to the King James Version, such as the Tyndale, Geneva, and Coverdale Bible. These have not enjoyed ongoing circulation like the King James Version. They did provide the basis for the King James text.[1] The versions before King James paved the way for the version accepted fully in the kingdom as the fulfillment of all the other versions.

1. The King James Version: its History and Usage

The King James Bible was authorized by James and translated by a translator's committee. The King James Version translated from the Greek version of the "Textus Receptus" text of the Septuagint. Catholicism has not tampered with these texts. It has the widest circulation of any Bible in history and has been the favorite translation of the Scripture of all time.[190] The King James Version of the Bible is the most popular version of all time, and it was the Bible the Pilgrims came with to the New World.

---

[189] Shelley, 313

[190] Sarah Pruitt, "Why the King James Bible of 1611 Remains the Most Popular Translation in History," Updated: July 13, 2023 Original: March 22, 2019, https://www.history.com/news/king-james-bible-most-popular, (Accessed November 18, 2024).

## 2. William Laud's Tyranny

To enforce his will upon the Puritans, the new King Charles found a ready servant in Archbishop William Laud (1573-1645), who believed God had ordained bishops to govern His Church. Led by the archbishop, an Episcopal party arose to resist the Puritans. They reintroduced stained glass windows, crosses, and even crucifixes with the King's support. They elevated the Communion table, called it an altar, and insisted that worship be conducted according to the Prayer Book and no other. Laud led a campaign to bring the State Church back to its Catholic moorings and sought to control it through the government, which would dictate what the congregations would do instead of being autonomous.

The straw that broke the back of restraint within the two kingdoms came when Charles tried to force his high church brand of Anglican religion upon the Presbyterian Scots. He insisted that they also conduct their worship services from the *Book of Common Prayer* there. John Milton called it 'the skeleton of a Mass book.' That is the way the Scots took it. They opposed the move and joined a 'National League of Covenant.' They dared to take up arms against their King to defend their Church.[191] This revolt against the King and Laud's demands was also a matter of patriotism; they resisted England from enforcing their will on Scotland, especially in matters of religion.

---

[191] Shelley, 315

The Scots were more hard-nosed than the Puritans in ways. The ministry of John Knox during Elizabeth's reign in England and Mary's (1542-1587) reign in Scotland solidified the country against Catholic practices and its control. Knox became the archenemy of Queen Mary. Knox and the Protestants won, and Mary fled to England, where Elizabeth imprisoned her and eventually had her beheaded.[192]

Laud's handling of the religious controversies in Scotland precipitated a civil war in England. He believed, as most men of that day still commonly believe, that one kingdom should have one religion or, at any rate, one Church. England and Scotland were now united under one King and should have a uniform religion. Each wished to impose its form of Protestantism upon the other. Laud took the initiative. The archbishop was not interested in requiring a subscription to the *Thirty-nine Articles*; he was willing to let the Scots believe as they would. But he insisted they conduct their services from *The Book of Common Prayer*.[193] This insistence of Laud was a play to get the religious state of both countries under royalty and a slap in the face of the Puritans, which would reap dire results.

Furthermore, The Prayer Book was built around the Christian year, which the Presbyterians and Puritans rejected. They said Christmas is "Christ-Mass, the devil with the sting in his tail."

---

[192] Latourette Vol. 2, 770-772
[193] Bainton vol. 2, 79-80

Away with Ash Wednesday, Lent, Easter, and all the holy days of Rome, which withdraw men from their godly callings! The Sabbath only, they insisted, was instituted by God and should be scrupulously observed on penalty of divine displeasure. When Archbishop Laud, in 1637, issued the order to the clergy of Scotland that they must use *The Book of Common Prayer*, a riot broke out in Edinburgh.[194] The very worship of the Puritans was mandated, and they felt helpless to oppose it because it meant fighting the power of the King and his government.

Other wars of religion were going on in Europe during England's troubles. The most devastating of the so-called wars of religion, the "Thirty Years War," began primarily as a religious struggle with political overtones and ended as a barbarous political power struggle with religious overtones. That shift in dominant motives makes the Thirty-Years War a fitting symbol of the transition from the Age of Reformation to the Age of Reason and Revivals.[195] The Puritans realized that Civil War was inevitable and could not be avoided. Forces released were impossible to reverse.

## C. The English Civil War

Charles (1600-1649), James' son, made one more fatal attempt to return the Church to Catholicism. He had a Catholic wife, the daughter of Philip of Spain. They secretly conspired to make England Catholic. The Puritans had enough by this

---

[194] Ibid
[195] Shelley, 321

time. They elected a leader, Oliver Cromwell (1599-1658), who engaged the King's army in civil war. Cromwell and his forces overruled the King. They entered London and dissolved Parliament.[196] The secret espionage to make England Catholic again infuriated the Puritans, who had grown in power and challenged the King and his forces.

The Army defeated the King's allies in early battles, and the Presbyterians were purged from the House of Commons. This so-called "Rump Parliament" – a tool of the Army – created a high court of justice to try the King.[197] The King had walked into a bee hive with the Puritans willing to take all means to punish him for what appeared to be "crimes against the state."

The Puritan's army was strong because of their leader. The increasing successes of the Parliamentary forces were largely due to the extraordinary abilities of Oliver Cromwell, who had risen to leadership of the Parliamentary armies. He resolved to have an army of saints, "men of spirit." Only such could stand against the sons of gentlemen who fought for the King. Social station was not to be regarded. "I had rather have a plain russet-coated captain that knows what he fights for and loves what he knows than that which you call a gentleman and is nothing else."[198] It seemed the Puritans represented the common man in

---

[196] Latourette, Vol 2, 821-823
[197] Ibid
[198] Bainton, Vol. 2, 81

Cromwell's army, and the elites comprised the King's armies.

Cromwell was not fatuous in looking upon the regiments thus recruited as Congregational Churches; their chaplains were Congregational ministers. A meeting of officers was conducted alternately as a debate and prayer meeting. Cromwell would sum up the sense of the meeting as if he were the clerk of the Society of Friends.[199] The army looked to God for victory over the King and his forces. They fought for their country to be free from tyranny.

Three years before the Battle of Dunbar, the King had surrendered to the Scots. Unable to agree with him, the Scots turned Charles over to the English. Cromwell favored the King's restoration until his deviousness came to light. The King's courier was intercepted, and his saddlebag was rifled. It contained correspondence with the Queen of Spain in which the King made it plain that he had no intention of keeping promises after he should have the power to break them. The King and Cromwell could not fathom each other. The King could not understand a man with no ambition and no point of corruption.[200] The secret plotting uncovered that the King could no longer reign in England. There seemed to be only one way to rid England of such foreign influence, or Spain would rescue the King and bring back Catholicism. It seemed hideous, but the action against the King

---

[199] Ibid, 82
[200] Ibid, 83-84

deemed it necessary. Shelley gives the beheading of the King by the Puritan's reasoning:

"The death sentence was pronounced on the King. He would be executed, with it being the only way to stop the agreement the King made with Spain to turn England Catholic after he was restored as King in January 1649. Charles was led to the scaffold in front of the royal palace of Whitehall in London, and before an assembled throng, he was executed. It was a brash move, a sure sign of Puritanism's ultimate fall from power, as some believed for it gave the royalists their own martyrs. Centuries of English royal tradition wouldn't be erased, even by the saints of God." [201]

Something like this had never happened in England and has never happened since. However, radical change appeared to occur, saving England from Catholicism.

The events ending the Civil War were rapid: The King was tried for conspiring with England's enemy and suffered a beheading. Cromwell was declared "Lord Protectorate" of England and ruled England for years in the name of God. His son, however, was weak, and England soon returned to a monarchy. [202] For over a decade, Cromwell ruled England in a way that had never been ruled before. He refused the address of the King, which made his reign different.

---

[201] Shelley, 317
[202] Latourette, Vol 2, 821-823

# D.  Cromwellian England

It was a new day for England because they had no King. The government was different from any other type England had ever had. England was now a theocracy. Cromwell abandoned a State Church to favor a national religion resting on Presbyterian, Independent, and Baptist pillars. They enjoyed full liberty, and he looked for full support from them.

Cromwell's second Parliament consisted of nominees from the independent congregations. It was called "The Barebones Parliament," from the name of one of its members. At its first session, Cromwell delivered a commission that sounded like an ordination sermon. As for the other groups, he applied Milton's theory of variety, which is restricted by the continuous theory of the two essentials. The Catholics and Unitarians were not to be tolerated. The Quakers were to enjoy the freedom of worship.[203]

Cromwell's reign had no complete religious freedom, but there was more freedom than was present under royalty. Bainton describes how Cromwell sought revenge on the Irish:

"Enemies who had aided the royalty in opposing the Puritans in the Civil War suffered punishment. The treatment of Ireland was brutal. Cromwell thought that eight years previously, the Irish "unprovoked had put the English to the most unheard of and most barbarous massacre (without

---

[203] Bainton, Vol. 2, 85

respect of sex) that ever the sun beheld." When Drogheda fell, the whole garrison was massacred. Cromwell's justification was that this bitterness will save much "effusion of blood," the current justification of those who extenuate the incineration of cities to shorten the war. Even greater resentment was occasioned in Ireland by the deportation of priests, the confiscation of estates, and the prohibition of the public exercise of Catholicism."[204]

Many believe this war against Ireland for their role against the Puritans in the Civil War was costly. Their support of Catholicism again in England made mortal enemies of the Irish and English that continue even to modern-day times.

Moral laws brought into effect during Cromwell's reign became common. Two notorious cases of blasphemy came up during the Protectorate. Blasphemy appeared more serious than heresy because of a public affront to the community's faith. Because of a heated public defense of his position, John Biddle, a Unitarian, was arrested under the Blasphemy Act.[205] Such rulings and punishment were deemed necessary for strict enforcement of a theocratic state.

Certain measures retained kept the government of England running. Direct taxation caused resentment among the saints. Another difficulty was that the revolution had been the army's work, and the army was loath now to

---

[204] Ibid
[205] Ibid

surrender in favor of Parliament. The army took over, and England was organized into districts under Major Generals.[206] Any top-heavy attempts to govern did not seem acceptable to those who had fought for the overthrow of the King and the Monarch he stood for. Cromwell grew old and died. His sons could not rule after him. England's experiment without a King was over.

F. The Restoration of the Monarchy

Charles II (1630-1685) was brought back from exile to assume the position of King. Cromwell's sons were not able to do so, and Parliament reinstated the office of King out of necessity.

Charles II's return was not accepted widely by dissenters from the Church of England. He banned those not affiliated with The Church of England from pulpits and Oxford. He even imprisoned many. Baptists were persecuted, and John Bunyan (1628-1688), a Baptist pastor, was jailed and wrote the great novel *Pilgrim's Progress*. The Tinker of Bedford was in prison for about 12 years in total.[207]

Charles enacted several restrictions and bans on groups during his reign. Eventually, they would be repealed, but caused havoc until that time. Milton's *Paradise Lost,* written by him in 1667, demonstrated with its release an indication of some

---

[206] Ibid, 87
[207] Nelson, Early Baptists, 404-405

loosening of restrictions on dissenters, notably Puritans.[208]

Charles made agreements with some groups that weakened his iron grip on the dissenters. He lived a loose life and eventually died a Catholic. His reign proved that a monarchy would not work in England regarding religion.[209]

When James II (1633-1701) succeeded his brother Charles II in 1685, he felt that the time had come for toleration; he, therefore, issued, in 1687, a Declaration of Indulgence, in which he candidly avowed his own adherence to the Church of Rome and his wish that all his subjects might be members of this communion.[210] England was through with Catholicism, though. His reign was short for his insistence on returning to Rome. Now, the stage was set for religious freedom for everyone.

## F. The Glorious Revolution

The freedom of religious groups to fully go public with their faith is the byproduct of the Act of Toleration, explained by Shelley:

"The denominational view of the Church found only limited acceptance in England, where the Church of England retained a favored position, even after the Act of Toleration. In 1689, though, the state recognized the right of Presbyterians,

---

[208] Adam Augustyn, Enclyopedia Britannica, John Milton,https://www.britannica.com/topic/Paradise-Lost-epic-poem-by-Milton. ND, (Accessed November 12, 2024).
[209] Nelson, Early Baptists, 276-283
[210] Bainton, Vol.2, 89

Congregationalists, Baptists, and Quakers to worship freely under William (1633-1701) and Mary (1662-1694), the new rulers. However, the denominational theory gained more acceptance in the English colonies of America. It seemed to be God's answer for the multiplying faiths in the New World."[211]

Within the denominational structure, groups could be identified, and power could be attained for their acceptance, although it came slowly for Baptists and other groups in the New World.

It was not an accident that the Great Awakening happened on both continents after the Glorious Revolution opened the door to preaching the gospel. Much of this openness came when religious discrimination was removed from groups not in the State Church. With the freedom to preach the gospel, Christianity thrived in the 18th Century. At the end of the 18th Century, the Great Mission movements and revivals reflect on this great decree and openness to the gospel.

The English stamp on the History of Christianity is vast. The newly settled colonies and the worldwide impact of the English Christian movement is far-reaching. The Baptist movement gained a foothold in America and England through the English Baptists. Other groups grew and prospered because of the rich history of the gospel freely preached after the two centuries of struggle for religious liberty. The steady influence of groups and individuals who have carried the gospel

---

[211] Shelley, 326

everywhere and established New Testament Churches has come from the English influence on Christianity.

# Chapter 16

# Puritanism and Its Influence
# 1580-1760

Of all the movements coming out of England, the Puritan movement probably had the most impact on the cause of Christ in England. The Puritans believed they could reform the Church of England and bring it out of the Catholic aspects of its makeup and practice. For two centuries, especially in 16th England, the Church of England went back and forth between these guideposts with its Catholic moorings and the Puritan movement to make the Bible the only source of faith and practice. A Civil War fought about the monarchy's power over the populace continued. The fight over when Charles I attempted to bring it back to Catholic practices brought tremendous division.

The Puritan movement was a movement spanning generations and leaders. They were not a flashing light but a religion of the common people fighting against a religion of the aristocrats represented in the royalty. Winning the Civil War brought Puritanism to its apex. Oliver Cromwell's reign was a victorious experience after he led the armies to win the Civil War. Although England returned to a monarchy, Puritanism's influence continued despite supposed setbacks.

The Puritan movement benefited through the Westminster Confession, which elaborated the core beliefs of Puritanism. Through this effort, a clear and certain reason for the Puritan movement was enunciated, and it helped understand what they believed in written form. These characteristics and people of Puritanism made it a lasting influence in England during turbulent times.

# A. Puritan Leaders and Their Contributions

The Puritan movement was progressive, eventually leading to a takeover of England and its government. Much of Calvin's views were alive in the Puritans. In its crusade to reshape England, the Puritan movement passed through three clearly marked periods: First, under Queen Elizabeth (1558-1603), it tried to "purify" the Church of England along the lines of Calvin's Geneva ministry. Second, under James I and Charles I (1603-1642), it resisted the claims of the monarchy and suffered under royal pressures designed to force conformity to a high church-style Christianity. Third, during England's Civil War and Oliver Cromwell's rule (1642-1660). Puritans had a chance to shape the national Church in England but failed because of their internal dissensions.[212] The lack of a strong

---

[212] Shelley, 310

successor to Cromwell killed the Puritan hold on the government. It also led to future clashes with the Royalty. Some see Puritanism as negative and controversial, while others see it as a moving force for reform and decency, as Shelley describes:

"Some look at Puritanism as the answer to other European countries' reformation. England's second Reformation first appeared during the reign of Elizabeth. It had a new style of preaching – a message aimed not at the head but at the heart. This "Spiritual brotherhood," as William Haller, the Puritan authority, once called it, includes names like Greenham, Rogers, Chaderton, and Dob. Many of these first Puritans had been Protestant exiles of the reign of Bloody Mary (1553-57). Hounded out of their homeland by their Catholic Queen, these Protestant sympathizers had gone to Geneva and mobilized as a vanguard for a fresh Calvinist assault on England."[213]

It was not the time to assert the Puritan's rise to power in Elizabeth's reign. However, their influence was beginning to grow. Puritanism's rise is because of several factors that spread to other countries and opposed affronts to New Testament Christianity. Bainton describes Puritanism's expansion:

"Puritanism could not be contained just to England. Of the main groups, one of the most important was that of the Presbyterians, which included the English and the Scottish Calvinists, who both objected to the imposition of episcopacy

---

[213] Ibid, 311

and *The Book of Common Prayer* by the Stuarts. Politically, they favored a constitutional monarchy. Their great proponent, Samuel Rutherford, wrote a book called Lex Rex, which means "the law is king," as opposed to rex lex, "the king is law."[214]

The monarchy was a huge barrier and enemy of the Puritan movement as the conflict increased.

# B. Strengths and Weaknesses of Puritanism

### 1. Its Strength

The Strength of Puritanism lies in its desire to get back to the basics of the Bible for Church belief and practice. They did not desire to break with the Church but to "purify" the Church. They longed for purity in doctrine and practice and wished to rid the Church of all doctrine and practice not in the Bible. The Puritans wanted to rid the Church of all false religious teachings. They were fond of referring to liturgical trappings of the Church as "taints of popery." The Puritans wanted the altar removed from worship and replaced with the Bible. They were instrumental in translating the King James Bible.[215] The Puritans were clear in what they opposed and the freedom they wanted given to them. Shelley describes the nexus of Puritanism when he shares:

"Puritanism has been falsely accused and also refuted by many. It is often generalized in an attempt to understand it. Early in the twentieth

---

214 Bainton, Vol 2, 72
215 Latourette, Vol 2, 813-815

century, American journalist H.L. Mencken summarized the popular image in his quip that Puritanism was "the haunting fear that someone, somewhere, may be happy." But is that fair? What was Puritanism originally? Whatever it was, it was not strait-laced. It stood for change and a new day in England. The first Puritans had little confidence in traditional religion. Their plans for a new England arose from a deep conviction that spiritual conversion was crucial to Christianity."[216]

The Puritan movement saw England growing out of royalty's control over the Church. However, the fight seemed to tighten between the two entities.

## 2. Its Weaknesses

The Puritans held to a Universal Church idea and tried to reform a corrupt institution when people needed a new one. They sought to control the government, which led to actual war, as in the case of Cromwell and his leadership.[217] Unlike the Separatists, they believed the government and church could be reformed without becoming a separate entity. They faced an increasing battle that led to war in their attempts that plunged England into turmoil.

---

[216] Shelley, 310

[217] John Briggs, "The Early English Baptists" *The History of Christianity*,: Oxford, England: Lion Publishers 1977 408-409.

# C. Puritanism's Tenets

The adoption of Confessions of Faith gave power to the Puritan movement. The Westminster Assembly, meeting from 1643 to 1649, produced *The Westminster Confession of Faith* to replace the Thirty-nine Articles and a Larger and Shorter Catechism for use in the churches. These writings alone made the assembly one of the most significant gatherings in Christian History. Many orthodox Presbyterians and Congregationalists use these documents to this day.[218] In a way, the Confession and its Assembly could be considered the alternative to the Council of Trent. At least, it defined the beliefs of the Puritan movement in England.

# D. Puritanism's Far-Reaching Effects

### 1. Its influences in England and America

Many Puritans fled to America, fed up with the civil strife in England, and deserted it. They established the Massachusetts Bay Colony. We know their influence on the "Puritan Work Ethic." They produced great pastors such as Jonathan Edwards. The Puritans had a deep desire for holiness and morality in the nation. They strongly influenced the formation of our nation through colleges and government and our first public school system. Those in England left their mark on the Church. The continual effort moved the Church from a political identity to a religious one, and they were instrumental in an "Act of Toleration" for all

---

[218] Shelley, 316

Churches in England.[219] The contributions of the Puritans were numerous and were especially evident in America.

2. The Prominent Exception to this General Policy of Religious Toleration was the Congregational Puritans of the Massachusetts Bay Colony.

They were determined to establish a new Zion in the American wilderness – a "due form of government both civil and ecclesiastical," as Governor John Winthrop put it.[220] The State Church was originally formed in certain colonies that did not offer complete tolerance to other dissenting groups like the Baptists.

3. A Second Check on Puritan Intolerance Hidden in the Wilderness.

Dissenters in New England did not need to go underground; they could move on – across the river, through the woods, or over the mountain. Sanctuary was always possible in an open space. Thus, Puritan devotion to the Bible, the presence of the wilderness, and the English policy of toleration combined to undercut the intolerance of the New England Puritans.[221] Certainly, the means of punishing dissenters were not as drastic and brutal as in the Mother Country. There were

---

[219]Emory Elliott, "The Legacy of Puritanism," https://nationalhumanitiescenter.org/tserve/eighteen/ekeyi nfo/legacy.htm., October 24, 2014, (Accessed October 25, 2024).
[220] Shelley, 323
[221] Ibid, 324

exceptions in some places, imprisoning Baptists and harassing them. However, this harassment was not as severe as England's clash.

Most of the basic beliefs of evangelicals could be found in Puritanism: The sinfulness of man, the atoning death of Christ, the unmerited grace of God, and the salvation of the true believer. But Puritanism was also concerned with politics. It tried to create the holy commonwealth, the true biblical society, in England and America.[222] Puritanism was not on the outside looking into basic Christian beliefs. The movement wanted those beliefs disseminated in the mainstream of government and culture.

Reformed Theology helped understand the Puritan movements by describing what the Bible taught. Particular Reformed Theology taught by Calvin greatly catapulted leaders into countries as John Knox did in Scotland. As these leaders went everywhere, so did the Word of God. It affected England so much that the King James Version appeased the Puritan leaders when King James, I endorsed it.

The common view of Puritans is unhappiness, and robbing others of happiness is an undeserved stereotype stuck in many quarters. But instead, the Puritans took stands, crossed the oceans, and settled here, never to go back. They also had joy in service of the Lord and their great

---

[222] Ibid, 351

exploits. Their high morality is still with us today, not for the worse but for the better.

# Chapter 17

# The Great Awakening Under George Whitefield's Leadership 1714-1770

The Great Awakening is one of the greatest periods in the History of Christianity. Despite much opposition from established churches, it featured many coming to Christ in repentance and faith on two continents. The Awakening stirred the souls of two nations and fueled future mission endeavors.

The need was great for Awakening with the new philosophies, the wars in the name of religion, and the partiality shown to the State Church of a country. America was trying to figure out if they wanted to be like England and have a state church discriminate against other groups not in the denomination that ruled as the State Religion of a certain colony. Yet, the Great Awakening looked beyond specific groups and led to the gospel being preached and the spirit being evident.

The 18th century brought peace from religious wars in Europe. However, God still needed to move people and churches out of their complacency toward fully understanding the gospel and the need to be born again. George Whitefield was greatly used to preach on both continents and see multitudes come to Christ, whether in church or in the open fields where he often preached. It was a new day for a somewhat complacent religion that now woke up in a way that could only be described as a tremendous outpouring of the Holy Spirit, resulting in multitudes coming into the Kingdom of God.

# A. The Need for Awakening

### 1. Religious Fighting

Countries had seen a very bad form of religion, with people killing one another because they were different. Catholics fought Protestants. The Thirty Years War was a religious war that ended in the "Peace of Westphalia." The "Act of Toleration" in England led to greater religious freedom there.[223] All this religious fighting caused great skepticism and people redefining the role of God in the world. This skepticism led to denying orthodoxy and rejecting the truth by focusing on the false. In the move to get away from corrupted religion, many settled for no religion at all.

---

[223] Latourette, vol 2, 887-889

Papal authority and enforcement of the State Religion were gone. The control of universal religion by the Pope was gone also. The Protestant Reformation led to a separation from the Church's ability to enforce religion. There was no complete separation of church and state. Some countries still enforced religion, but not to the extent done before the Reformation.[224] There was greater freedom to display doubts and pessimism about religion and to deny the supernatural aspect of religion.

2. Scientific Discovery

Science is not an enemy of religion, but it was perceived to be so by religion in light of some of the first discoveries. The Catholic Church had opposed some of Galileo's ideas about the universe. Other opposition led many to believe that science and the Bible were incompatible. This skepticism led many who made scientific discoveries to reject religion. They thought that to believe in science meant an automatic rejection of religion.[225] For those unfamiliar with the Bible or arguments for its validity, the scientific discoveries challenged them. They left many denying the role of religion in the history of the world and its study.

3. Enlightenment of Man through Education

The Renaissance had brought about a rebirth of study in the classics. A Renaissance man typically thought for himself and was not bound to the past. Since religion represented the past, the

---

[224] Ibid, vol. 2, 980
[225] Ibid,

truths of the Christian faith skeptically led to denying them.[226] In many cases, there was a conflict with the Church, viewing the Church as the old guard and relic of the Dark Ages.

Assurances of orthodoxy did not seem too certain. A man was defied through humanism. The divine right of kings was suspect. Philosophers like Rosseau stood for the freedom of man to control his own destiny. This questioning led to a philosophy called Deism, which invaded England and even America. It said God wound up the world like a clock and left it alone, and we certainly cannot know God that personally.  With the responsibility to God removed, it led to an increase in immorality.[227] With a lack of Christian ethics, the alternative was to deny the reason for moral behavior that was in tune with Scripture.

According to the Enlightenment leaders, several harsh spinster nannies had confined thinkers to an intellectual nursery in previous centuries. These were the Church, the Bible, creeds, tradition, old scientific theories, the emperor, and the Pope. But now, humanity has grown up and can think and explore independently. The motto of Immanuel Kant (1724-1804) was a call for bravery to break away from the nannies: "Dare to know! Have the courage to use your understanding."[228] Self-study and a rejection of accepted beliefs about God and religion increased

---

226 Bainton, Vol 2, 110
227 Ibid, Vol. 2, 111-115
228 Bingham, 132

through philosophies that continued to change the public, particularly in higher education.

Faith in this new age was not the starting point for philosophy. Anselm prayerfully confessed, "I believe so that I may understand," the rationalists declared, "I understand to believe." And the empiricists proclaimed, "I experience to believe." And the scientific revolution announced, "We calculate to believe." The inspired teaching of the apostle Paul – "Faith comes from hearing, and hearing through the Word of God" (Romans 10:14) was the biblical starting point for believing.

Faith is being certain of something without sensory experience, without seeing, touching, hearing, or feeling it. And faith is the basis of understanding. It is not that understanding is a prerequisite for faith.[229] For Christians, faith must come first to make sense of the world's existence and order.

New ways of viewing biblical truths changed how many believed in traditional teaching. In addition to eroding divine revelation as the foundation of faith and mocking tradition, the Enlightenment challenged several Christian doctrines. Jeffery Bingham enumerates this kind of refusal:

"First, rather than affirming the doctrine of original sin, the Enlightenment denied it and stressed that the idea was oppressive. Humanity, they believed, needs to be set free not from sin but

---

[229] Ibid, 134

from belief in original sin. Second, rather than affirming the reality of a fallen world tragically affected by sin, Enlightenment people said natural disasters mean that a merciful, sovereign, divine being does not exist or at least is not involved in the world. Third, they said the Bible is merely a collection of documents without the quality of inspiration. Since the Bible has no divine authorship, it is interpreted like any other worldly literature. Fourth, the Enlightenment maligned the person of Jesus Christ. Fifth, the Enlightenment leaders twisted the doctrine of salvation, Christ's work on the cross. They said Christ did not die in our place for the penalty of our sins."[230]

Such reasoning removed man's responsibility to God for His eternal soul and guidance.

These ideas affect the thinking of modern man. He says, "The spirit of the Enlightenment didn't disappear; it is still with us today. It has influenced everything in the modern world, even many Christians and churches. Since the eighteenth century, Western culture, in its approach to truth, has been dramatically characterized by the emphases found in the Enlightenment."[231] It is a tragedy that the same spirit could not be utilized to understand the Scriptures more and not reject its truths so easily. Bingham continues to explain:

The Reformation truths were no longer new for most of Europe. The Enlightenment eventually

---

[230] Ibid, 135-136
[231] Ibid, 136

cooled the fires of the Reformation in Europe. But amid the Age of Reason, the Reformation was already cooling for other reasons. The primary reason was formalism. Thus, two arrows had pierced the chest of the Reformation: reason and ritual. It was popular to believe that salvation was simply a matter of giving assent to orthodox beliefs or behaving morally.[232]

The emphasis denounced the atoning work of Christ on the cross and favored a religion of man-made effort that looks to self-enlightenment and behavior as his home for civility in the world. This thinking ignored Luther's truth that "The Just shall live by Faith."

The denial of any supernatural religion highlighted the Age of Reason. Respect for science and human reason replaced the Christian faith as the cornerstone of Western culture. Many Protestants met this crisis of faith not by arguments but by the experience of supernatural conversion.[233] This "crisis" was met with the revival of preaching the Bible and evangelistic efforts that would bring those left outside the Church into the Kingdom of God. This revival would see the gospel preached clearly by his willing instruments. Shelley reasons:

The old vanguard of commonly accepted religious truths was less prevalent with the Enlightenment. Christians found themselves in two contrasting climates. At first, during the closing

---

[232] Ibid, 137
[233] Shelley, 327

years of the seventeenth century, some believers, especially in England, tried to harmonize reason and faith. They argued that Christianity is totally reasonable, but some truths come by reason and some by revelation. However, after the beginning of the eighteenth century, the climate changed. In France, confidence in reason soared, and Christians found that many intellectuals dismissed all appeals to revealed Scripture as superstitious nonsense.[234]

Yet, with the void, there was a stirring of hunger, not just human reason to decide man's fate but to look to the Scripture for hope and salvation.

Interestingly, many still believed in a higher power, but they seemed to redefine who He was. Curiously enough, atheism was not fashionable in this "polite society." Most of the prominent "infidels" who ridiculed Christianity during the eighteenth century believed in a "Supreme Being" but regarded it superstitious to hold that he interfered with the world machine. This belief was called deism.[235] His intervention was about to take the form of awakenings toward Christianity, not to be dismissed.

## B. Whitefield's Conversion and Ministry

George Whitefield stands at the forefront of the Great Awakening Movement. Some believe there would be no Great Awakening without God using him to bring revival. In the preaching tours

---

[234] Ibid, 333
[235] Ibid, 334

of George Whitefield (1714-1770) during the 1740s, sleepy souls of New England were led into full spiritual consciousness. In particular, during 1740, Whitefield preached 175 sermons to thousands in a marathon forty-five-day itinerant preaching tour. This wonderfully gifted Calvinistic speaker could attract and hold the attention of virtually anyone. Preferring narrative portions of Scripture, Whitefield painted captivating, imaginative word pictures of heaven, hell, humanity's desperate need for Christ, and conversion through faith as the dramatic change in one's affections and life orientation from self to God.[236] Whitefield took both continents by storm and was the first evangelist/preacher to have a sustained ministry in these two continents.

America saw gospel preachers who went everywhere preaching the gospel to accompany Whitefield. The winds moved on to the Scotch-Irish Presbyterians in the area. In the little school, dubbed a "Log College" by more bookish clergymen, a Pennsylvania preacher named William Tennent started turning out a number of ministers with "evangelical zeal." His alumni soon had the winds of revival whipping through a number of churches, particularly in New Jersey. In a short time, a controversy arose over the question of "educated" versus "converted" ministers, and the whole Presbyterian Church divided into "New Side" men, favoring the revival, and "Old Side" men opposing it.[237] The distinction was stark, and

---

[236] Bingham, 138-139
[237] Shelley, 364

the awakenings broke out throughout the countryside.

Whitefield and Tennett's son Gilbert preached in meetings together throughout New England. They were well received and worked to keep the revival fires continuing.[238]

The beginnings of George Whitefield were humble. Raised at a tavern in Gloucester, England, he entered Oxford and associated with John and Charles Wesley and the "Holy Club," who did charitable deeds for others. His born-again experience came to him through much study and deprivation by reading Henry Scrogal's *The Life of God in the Soul of Man*. Whitefield was converted to Christ there and devoted the rest of his life to preaching the gospel.[239]

Whitefield went where John Wesley had failed to establish an orphanage called Bethesda in the virgin colony of Georgia, just being settled by individuals from debtors' prisons. On his return trip to America, he preached to huge crowds in New England, befriending Gilbert Tennett, Benjamin Franklin, and Jonathan Edwards.[240]

In England, Whitefield began to attract large crowds in churches, and God placed upon his heart a burden for the masses who never went to a Church. He began to preach to the miners at

---

[238] Dan Nelson, *A Burning and Shining Light: The Testimony and Witness of George Whitefield*. (Lifesong Publishers Somis, CA, 2017) ,77.
[239] Ibid, 28-34
[240] Ibid, 80-92

Kingswood Colliers, outside of Bristol. Whitefield preached to the miners coming to and from the mines. As opposition arose from the liberal clergy, he began to preach in the open air and attracted thousands of people to hear him preach. Multitudes experienced conversion, and revival began to break out in England.[241]

## C. Whitefield's Preaching and Impact

Calvinism influenced Whitefield, and he broke with Wesley over Arminianism.[242] Whitefield continued preaching in America and later died there preaching. He had made seven trips to America from England, unheard of at that time and age.[243]

Whitefield was the first mass evangelist. He was one of the most influential and effective evangelists. His dramatic style of delivery caused many to consider Christ. He encouraged John Wesley, although differing from him in theology, to preach to the masses. God used him as one of the greatest preachers of all time.[244]

Whitefield was well received in America and made friends with Jonathan Edwards, a Congregational Pastor and Puritan in Northampton, Massachusetts. The town experienced a great

---

[241] Ibid, 65-67

[242] Ibid, 100-101

[243] Peter James Hoffer, *When Benjamin Franklin Met The Reverend Whitefield: Enlightenment, Revival and the Power of the Printed Word* (John Hopkins University Press: Baltimore 2011), 272

[244] Nelson, A Burning and Shining Light, 263

revival under Edwards and a second great movement of God under Whitefield's preaching.[245]

Most Americans are estimated to have heard Whitefield preach personally in the colonies at one time or another. The announcement that Whitefield would preach brought a flurry of activity as people ran to listen to him preach the unsearchable riches of Christ.[246]

Whitefield preached over 18,000 sermons in 34 years, crisscrossing the countryside of England and America, establishing friends, and ushering many thousands into the Kingdom of God. Without Whitefield's preaching, there would be no Great Awakening as we know it.[247]

D. Chronology of Whitefield's Life

1. Childhood and Upbringing (1714-1732)

Whitefield grows through adversity when working with his family at the Bell Inn. He excels in drama and earns a servitor position at Oxford University.

2. School, Conversion, and Call to Ministry (1732-1737)

Whitefield joins the Holy Club led by John Wesley. He seeks a relationship with God and finds

---

[245] Ibid, 87-90

[246] George Whitefield: Did You Know

https://christianhistoryinstitute.org/magazine/article/george -whitefield-did-you-know, N.A, Article in Christian History magazine, Issue 38, 1993. (Accessed, November 22, 2024),

[247] Fish, Bruce and Becky. *George Whitefield, Pioneering Evangelist* (Barbour Books: Uhrichsville, OH, 2000),280.

Christ in the new birth experience after a desperate struggle with God. Whitefield returns to Gloucester to recover from health problems and feels called to preach. He is ordained and begins his preaching ministry.

3. Call to America and Beginning of a Ministry (1738-1739)

Whitefield goes to Georgia to understand the needs of the new colony. He determined to get sponsorship from the trustees of the Parliament in England for an orphanage. He begins a successful ministry in Bristol among miners while waiting to go to Georgia.

4. Ministry in America (1739-1740)

The Bethesda Orphanage begins. Whitefield preaches in New England and at Jonathan Edward's Church in Northampton, Massachusetts. Thousands flock to hear him. He preaches in Philadelphia, where Benjamin Franklin becomes a lifelong friend. He also preaches with Gilbert Tennant, an American Itinerant Evangelist.

5. Return to England, Marriage, and Preaching in Scotland (1741-1744)

Whitefield returned to England to be a leader of the Calvinistic Methodist Movement. He marries Elizabeth James. They have their only son, who died at four months of age. Under Whitefield's preaching, a Great Awakening breaks out in Cambuslang, Scotland.

6. American Victories and the Growth of Bethesda (1744-1748)

Whitefield preaches in New England again, sponsored by Benjamin Franklin, and oversees the work at Bethesda. He became America's most famous and captivating preacher of the era and was a loving ambassador for Bethesda, the orphanage he founded.

7. Trials and Tribulations in England and More Ministry in America (1748-1755)

Opposition arises to Whitefield's ministry. Attacks and threats to his life are faced. The work prospers with Lady Huntingdon's sponsorship, the Tabernacle's building, and other preaching spots. He returns to America on his fourth and fifth preaching tours.

8. Physical Illness and Ministry in England delaying return to America (1756-1763)

Travels have worn Whitefield out. Prevented from going to America because of the Seven-Year War, he seeks physical recovery. His tabernacle expanded, with the Tottenham Chapel built for his preaching.

9. More Physical Difficulties and Loss of Wife (1763-1768)

Whitefield makes his sixth voyage to America after the war. He is honored by Yale University with an M.A. degree. Whitefield has to rest more and begins to train others to take over his ministry. His wife dies, and he preaches her funeral.

10. Final Trip to America and Entrance into Glory (1769-1770)

Whitefield is honored at Bethesda and preaches for the last time in New England. He was very ill, dying in Newburyport, Massachusetts. His funeral service was at the Presbyterian Church in Newburyport, Massachusetts, and he is buried in a vault in the basement under the pulpit area.[248]

One could only imagine what it was like to hear Whitefield preach to the tremendous crowds that came to listen to him. His booming voice penetrated the outside darkness like a lightning bolt. No other preacher of his time had such an impact on an audience based on all the churches and ministries established through him. The number of relationships built on both continents allowed the Awakening to prepare Americans for the Revolution against England. The Awakening, in a way, unified the American Colonies spiritually. It also saw whole nations alive with spiritual fervor through Whitefield's ministry.

Whitefield boldly went where no one had before. He was sometimes willing to risk his life for the furtherance of the gospel and the open doors God gave him. Those who followed him were amazed at how God used him and carried on the revival torch, so to speak. In a way, Whitefield's ministry made both continents biblically literate again. It brought religion to the forefront of matters, whether in the beginnings of the Revolutionary War or in the places of England where the gospel went forth in mighty power. Its preaching produced a new spirit that brought many souls into the Kingdom of God.

---

[248] All information covered in these episodes of Whitefield's life are recorded in my book, *A Burning and Shining Light: The Testimony and Witness of George Whitefield.*

# Chapter 18

## The Great Awakening under Jonathan Edwards and John Wesley's Leadership

As a movement, the Great Awakening first broke out in Northampton, Massachusetts, in the Congregational Church under Johnathan Edwards, its pastor. He was hardly the candidate for God to use, but he was the one who led his congregation to see all that God could do. In 1735, what broke out in the Church spilled over to the entire community and area. The movement saw containment there but eventually came to all of New England.

A visit by George Whitefield to Edward's Church in 1740 produced another great move of

God. Spiritual conversation and conversion were throughout the town. Whitefield returned to England with memories of the open doors, fellow companionship of Edwards, and their availability to be used by God. Opposition broke out in the movements, but in America, Edwards explained it in several works, particularly *Narrative of the Surprising Work of God*, a recording of all God had done.[249]

Now, the expectation in America was more than just for a place to worship, but an interruption to a way of life that was heaven-sent. Edwards and John Wesley in England were at the center of all that God did.

## A. Revival in Northampton, Massachusetts, under Edwards' Leadership

Jonathan Edwards (1703-1758) was trained at Yale and was a product of a minister's home. He articulated what God was doing in the Awakening. Edwards was one of the greatest theologians America has ever produced. He pastored at Northampton for 23 years. But his influence went far beyond there into all of New England. A sermon, "Sinners in the Hands of an Angry God," preached at Enfield, Connecticut, brought the whole town to a standstill, resulting in the conversions of many youth signed up for membership by their parents

---

[249] Jonathan Edwards, revised and corrected by Edmund Hickman, *The Works of Jonathan Works*, (The Banner of Truth Trust: Carlisle, PA, reprinted 1984),344-364.

in the Halfway Covenant but unconverted. Massive repentance and awakening broke out all over.[250]

Edwards devoted 13 hours daily to study, and his home was a model one. He had a monotone voice and poor eyesight. He read sermons, but God used them to bring great revival. After a 23-year pastorate, a Lord's Supper debate led to a controversy that broke out. The disagreement led to Edwards's dismissal from his Church, which related to the candidates for the Lord's Supper.[251]

Edwards was a missionary to the Indians in Stockbridge for seven years after his time at Northampton. He had earlier published an account of missionary efforts by David Brainard, who died at a young age while trying to preach to the Native Americans and being engaged to Edward's daughter, Jerusha. Brainard's full potential was largely unknown to the world. Still, Edwards published his diary to help people understand his sacrifices for bringing the gospel to the local Native Americans.

The Awakening in Northampton led to an era of mass conviction. "The Spirit of God began extraordinarily to set in." Edwards reported, "A great and earnest concern about the great things of the eternal world swept the town. There was scarcely a single person in the town, old or young, left unconcerned about the great things of the

---

[250] Iain, H. Murray, *Jonathan Edwards, A New Biography* (Banner of Truth Trust, Carlisle, PA, 1987), 168-171.
[251] George Marsden, *Jonathan Edwards, A Life.* (Yale University Press New Haven, CT, 2003.), 183.

eternal world...The work of conversion was carried on in a most astonishing manner; as it were, souls came by flocks to Jesus Christ."[252] These were true marks of an awakening of spiritual religion. It caused even the stoic Edwards to be excited about what the Lord was doing. Shelley explains the new light of the Awakening leaders:

"This "new light" or "inward witness" was the key to the revival in New England. The revivalists pointed out that their fathers had left the Church of England to come to America precisely because they believed it was contrary to the Word of God to permit the unconverted to enter into Church membership. The Awakening, they felt, was a call from God to begin a 'new reformation' in New England. Thus, "New Lights began separating from parish churches and organizing their own congregations using the methods of the founding fathers of New England."[253]

The Revival became a wake-up call to an institutional religion involving most colonies. The New Lights had been awakened and wanted the whole neighborhood to do the same. It was not a preference to be personally right with God but a necessity.

Shelley shares, "Edwards was a very learned pastor, as demonstrated in his writing and preaching. The revivalists, though appealing to the masses, were not unobstructed. Jonathan Edwards had sound knowledge of the science of Newton and

---

[252] Shelley, 366
[253] Ibid, 357

the philosophy of Locke, while John Wesley was widely read."[254] The Awakening preachers such as Edwards were not uneducated men; neither were they men who lacked an understanding of the current philosophical trends and works in the secular arena. Shelley illumines about the dangers of the Halfway Covenant:

A second level of church membership devised by creating ecclesiastical societies to handle temporal affairs led to future problems. Solomon Stoddard, the grandfather of Jonathan Edwards, was even ready to go as far as to admit the unconverted to Communion in the hope of their conversion. But, vastly better would it be to convert the entire community. In that case, the church, state, and community would be bound in a bond of grace, and the Holy Commonwealth would become such a reality as it had never been. This setup was Jonathan Edwards's hope.[255]

Edwards did not want Northampton to be an isolated island. He wrote and traveled across colonies to Enfield, Connecticut, in 1741, where he preached the famous sermon "Sinners in the Hands of an Angry God."

Edwards read in the message from Scripture about the way the Bible describes Hell and eternal destruction. He described the peril of the lost in picturesque examples of many persons and animals in danger. As he later described these in great realism, those in the congregation began to

---

[254] Bainton, vol. 2, 114
[255] Ibid, 126

clutch the pillars of the church building for fear of slipping into eternal destruction. The sermon resulted in the conversion of many. However, this sermon was not typical of Edward's usual sermons. To portray him simply as dangling sinners over the pit of hell is to countenance one of the travesties of history.[256] This sermon was an inaccurate picture of his whole ministry at the time. Although this subject fits the occasion of Edwards delivering it, it is not a typical picture in the panorama of his sermons.

Edwards had a heart for people to be born-again. He set out to see the entire community converted. That Edwards should ever have supposed this goal may appear fatuous, seeing that Edwards believed in predestination. Edwards would have only the elect as members of the church, but he wanted everyone to be elect. At any rate, the preacher must proffer God's grace, for God has ordained preaching as how to disclose to the elect, and who was the preacher to assume that any in his congregation were not?[257] Edwards did not believe in the fatalistic view of Calvinism that many associate with that theology. Instead, he believed in the calling out of the elect through preaching the gospel and the fruits they would display of true conversion.

Edwards believed that "spiritual knowledge," or knowledge of Jesus' identity as Christ, the Son of God, had no human messenger. God alone is its author by the revealing ministry of the Spirit of

---

[256] Ibid, 127
[257] Ibid

God. A person may become religiously interested because of the message spoken by another person, but this would not be "spiritual light" or "spiritual discovery." When one has been "spiritually enlightened," a heart and mind transformation occurs.[258] The newness of spiritual birth accompanied a desire to love the things of God and a spiritual growth in the people of God.

## B. Edwards' Influence in America Through His Writing and Leadership

Edwards became president of Princeton, but unfortunately, he was only there for six months, dying at the school because of a smallpox epidemic and vaccination he took to try and guard against its ravaging effect.[259] The Awakening under his and other's leadership saved America from destruction and positioned the country to become a great nation.

Conversion, viewed through its totality, became the important center of the Awakening. Conversion to Edwards was not just expressing faith in Christ as the only thing required to be a Christian. Conversion is not about merely "getting saved"; it is not simply uttering a short prayer. Conversion is a new, enlightened, and true way of seeing God and his Word. And this way of seeing God comes only from Him. And yet, for Edwards, such faith, such a conversion of mind and heart, is not irrational.[260] Edwards indicated that a desire for

---

[258] Bingham, 139
[259] Murray, 441
[260] Ibid, 140

the will of God in one's life comes through conversion and the Spirit's leadership in your life. Bingham helps understand the effects of the Awakening that Jonathan Edwards believed:

"The definition of Revival can be seen clearly in what happened at Northampton. Edwards also addressed the signs of a true revival. In the treatise *The Distinguishing Marks of a Work of the Spirit of God* (written in 1741, the same year as his famous sermon "Sinners in the Hands of an Angry God." Edwards identified several criteria for authentic awakening based on I John 4:1-21. A true work of God's Spirit does not mean a person's conversion becomes instantly or is totally holy. Edwards pointed out five clear evidences of actual conversion: (1) a conviction that Jesus is the incarnate, virgin-born, crucified Son of God and Savior of sinful humans (1 Jn 4:2-3); (2) a developing disinterest in, and a weaning away from worldly lusts and pursuits, accompanied by an affection for the supremacy of things divine and heavenly (1 Jn 4:4-5); (3) an appreciation and higher regard for the Scriptures, (1 Jn 4:6); (4) a truthful view of things regarding God, sin and self (1 Jn 4:6); and (5) a growing love for God and fellow humans (1 Jn 4:7-21)."[261]

These tests indicate what God did and is doing in one's life when conversion to Christ occurs and the results of such a conversion.

Edwards continued to write about the Awakening. He was an on-the-spot reporter. Perhaps

---

[261] Ibid, 140-141

Edwards' most developed understanding of the essence of spiritual revival is presented in his work *A Treatise Concerning Religious Affections*, written in 1746. There, he stated, "True religion, in great part, consists in holy affections." By "affections," he meant the virtues imparted to us supernaturally through the indwelling of the Holy Spirit, what Paul called "the fruit of the Spirit."[262] These fruits of the Spirit are evident and purposeful in one's life, truly converted. The affection for the things of God and His truth in His word will be apparent to the converted and those who see their life.

We can see from these glances at the teachings of Jonathan Edwards that he was a theologian of revival. Careful doctrinal contemplation of how God works in revival, what revival consists of, and where it should lead did not get buried in the revival drama.[263] True revival is beyond feeling but an inspiration to live a Godly life and influence others.

There were some physical manifestations in Northampton and the revival of the area. Some questioned their validity. Edwards replied that physical manifestations neither prove nor disprove the reality of a religious experience; the test lies in the fruit of the Spirit.[264] Public testimony proven by one's changed life, not just words, indicates true salvation.

Understanding Edwards is crucial to understanding his impact on the Awakening. Later

---

[262] Ibid,141
[263] Ibid, 142
[264] Bainton, Vol. 2, 130

generations of Americans almost forgot that Edwards was a keen psychologist, a brilliant theologian, and the third president of Princeton. They remembered him, inaccurately, only as one more dramatic preacher of hellfire and brim-stone.[265] This characterization is unfortunate since he excelled in many areas of writing and being a pastor. He is a respected theologian who should be acknowledged as that by all today.

## C. Wesley's Background and Conversion

### 1. Home and Education

John Wesley (1703-1791) far outlived George Whitefield and led a great awakening in England. He was a persistent organizer, and not as dramatic a preacher as Whitefield. His followers, known for their methodical ways, earned the name "Methodist."[266] The Methodists lived and preached consistently to reflect the life of Christ in them.

Wesley was the son of a minister who had 14 children. His mother, Susannah, devoted an hour a week to the spiritual training of each child. At Oxford,

---

[265] Shelley, 367

[266] Andrew Schleicher "Why the Wesley's, and others, came to be called Methodists," https://www.umc.org/en/content/why-the-wesleys-and-others-came-to-be-called- methodists#: ~:text=%22These%20were%20all%20names%20foisted, and%20updated%20June%2028%2C%202023, September 21, 2015, and updated June 28, 2023, (Accessed, October 28, 2024).

he organized the Holy Club.[267] This group had notable students; not the least was George Whitefield, who was converted there in Oxford, as has already been revealed.

2. Wesley spent his early life as an unconverted minister.

He went to Georgia as a missionary but exclaimed, "I went to Georgia to convert the heathen, but oh, who shall convert me?" On his initial trip to Georgia aboard a ship, he encountered a storm and witnessed the peace of the Moravians they had in the storm. They told him of the new birth, which brought him under conviction of his religious but unconverted condition."[268] Wesley's state at this time warns all that they may know scriptural truths and not respond to them. They may substitute a moral life and moral character but may miss the important truths of salvation until they face it and understand it.

## D. Wesley's Impact on England and Methodism

### 1. Conversion

Back in England after his unsuccessful ministry in Georgia, Wesley gave testimony to his conversion on May 24, 1738, which took place during the reading of *Luther's Preface to his Commentary of Romans*. He heard Peter Bohler

---

[267] Latourette, Vol 2, 823

[268] Arnold A. Dallimore, *George Whitefield: God's Anointed Servant in the Great Revival of the Eighteenth Century*, Vol. 1. (Crossway: Wheaton, Ill., 1990), 141-145.

share this message in a Moravian chapel on Fetter Lane. It resulted from the Moravians following up on him and getting him under the preaching of the gospel. His conversion reflects these themes through the experience of grace guiding him to dedicate himself to the work of evangelism in order to bring divine light to human souls.[269] This moving testimony revealed what Wesley was missing. However, he was raised in a minister's home, trained spiritually by his mother, and even served as a missionary and pastor before his conversion.

### 2. Beginnings of Ministry

Wesley began to preach in the open field and adopted Arminianism as a theology. He organized converts into societies for continued religious instruction. He said he began to "look upon the world as his parish" and devoted more time to preaching than probably any other preacher. He died at 88, and the Methodist Church was formed shortly after his death.[270] The high churchman looked now upon the world as His mission field and beyond the church building into the deepest places of society.

Wesley's tradition continued in America with the preaching of Francis Asbury. His brother Charles wrote many hymns for the Awakening. The

---

[269] Kidd, Thomas S. *George Whitefield: America's Spiritual Founding Father*. Yale University Press: New Haven, CT, 2014), 50-51.

[270] Skevington Wood, John and Charles Wesley, *History of Christianity*,: Oxford, England: Lion Publishers 1977) 456-457.

Wesleyan movement gave rise to many other movements, such as the abolition of slavery.[271] The movement was concerned with saving the culture and not just the saving of souls. The saving of souls opened the door to even greater needs and issues.

### 3. Impact of the Wesleyan Revivals

The Wesleyan Revivals saved England from moral chaos and anarchy that gripped France. Someone said, "While heads were rolling from the guillotine in the French Revolution, people were bowing at the foot of the cross in England." [272]

When the hardened miners of Bristol pled for God's mercy in such great numbers, Whitefield urged Wesley to follow his lead into the open fields. John knew he was no match for Whitefield's oratory. "Having been so tenacious of every point relating to decency and order all my life," he wrote, "I should have thought the saving of souls almost a sin if it had not been done in a church."[273] Wesley has Whitefield to thank for his first congregation among the miners at Kingswood Colliers out of Bristol. Whitefield literally gave him the congregation he had built by preaching to the miners, who went to work in the morning and returned that night. He returned to America as

---

[271] Ibid
[272] Stephen Flick, "The Prayer Meeting that Saved England, Christian History Magazine," (https://christianheritagefellowship.com/prayer-meeting-that-saved-england/, December 27, 2023, (Accessed October 27, 2024).
[273] Shelley, 356

Wesley inherited his congregation and for even greater exploits.

Wesley believed in a gracious restoration of free will within fallen humanity and was convinced that redeemed humans were capable of a level of perfect sanctification in this life.[274] This led some down the path to what they surmised was "sinless perfection," although it was not mostly characteristic of the Wesleyan revival and his beliefs. Shelley describes Wesley's leadership in Revival throughout England:

"The Wesleyan Revival started as a Church Revival. Most of the believers in the Wesleyan Revival were members of the Anglican Church, and Wesley urged them to attend their parish Churches for worship and Holy Communion. He was still the devout churchman from Epworth Rectory. But his converts found the center of their Christian experience in the Methodist societies where they confessed their sins to one another, submitted to the discipline of their leader, and joined in prayer and song."[275]

Wesley did not try to start another denomination. He and Whitefield remained loyal to the Church, though the denomination did not agree with much of its methods of reaching the lost.

---

[274] Bingham, 143
[275] Shelley, 358

# E.  Lasting Results in England of Wesley's Ministry

Roland Bainton said, "Wesley did more to make England Puritan (or Biblical Christians) by conversion than the Puritan movement ever had done by force of arms.[276] His ministry was non-violent, and he knew people and culture would be changed not by laws or political movements but by people converted through preaching the gospel and people's reception of it.

Wesley had a colorful ministry that he described in his diary, which he meticulously kept. In his diary, Wesley records that once, he was riding in a coach when the mob began pelting it with stones. A large gentlewoman then sat in his lap and shielded him. Frequently, he quieted mobs by his sheer intrepidity. Once, he was besieged in a house. The leader of a gang broke into his room just as the doors were shut, holding back the rest of the mob. A missile came through and hit the ruffian. He bellowed, "What shall we do?" "Pray, man!" said Wesley, and he did. Many disturbers were so moved by Wesley's composure as to turn suddenly on the assailants and defy anyone to touch him.[277]

Wesley was fearless as a preacher, although his life was threatened on several occasions. He stood courageous against such attacks as did

---

[276] Bainton, Vol.2, 122
[277] Ibid, vol 2, 123

Whitefield and trusted in the Lord for his protection.

The preacher was well acquainted with the English countryside. Bainton said, "No one in his century knew the British Isles so intimately, and his journal is one of the great social documents of the century. At the end of his long career, when he returned to places where he once got mobbed, the crowds hailed him as if he had been King George.[278] His travels all over England by horseback, and the assistants he sent out gave him a great knowledge of the culture and a working knowledge of where everything was.

Wesley left a legacy after he died by crossing all over England, preaching the gospel, and establishing societies. These societies eventually became the basis for the Methodist Church after he died. The continual evangelistic work done was a reason for the rapid growth of Methodism in England and America.[279] Although he did not try to start a new denomination, it would inevitably happen since the staid majority in the Church of England would not adopt Wesley's method and energy to reach people for Christ.

The life and ministry of John Wesley and his fellow ministers are forever etched in the fabric of Evangelical Christianity. The Methodist Church directly resulted from his ministry in England and America. It is interesting how the Awakening under

---

[278] Ibid, 123

[279] Wood, "John and Charles Wesley", *History of Christianity*, 456-457

Wesley's leadership spilled over to the culture and worked through the movement to realistically move England past losing their colonies to a new nation protected from the horrors of the French Revolution.

Modern denominations and churches need to turn the page back to the Great Awakening movement and see how God used its leaders so mightily. The outpouring of the Spirit was not entertainment in the Church but a rescuing of a culture doomed to break apart into listlessness. Yet, God intervened and worked through them, stepping in and using men like Edwards and Wesley to see revival in churches and Spiritual Awakening in nations.

# Chapter 19

# Religious Liberty and Its Influence in America

The wars engendered by the State Church, religion, and the revivals that broke out in the Great Awakening caused America as a new nation to look closely at the role of Christianity in government. Certainly, our founders, for the most part, put Christianity at the center of their lives, looking for worship and leadership from God in establishing a new nation. The Declaration of Independence testifies to this truth with the strong reliance on God for the new nation's freedom.

Favoritism toward the colony's dominant denomination and persecution toward other groups not in the State Religion of a colony called for change. A new perspective on how religious liberty for all religious groups should be a reality. A strong push from pastors under the leadership of John Leland, a pastor in Virginia, cried for this discrimination to end. He wanted a codification of religious liberty in the nation's new Constitution. It is imperative to understand religious liberty and how it pertains specifically to the United States of America.

# A. Early Influences on Religious Liberty

## 1. State Religion by Colonies

Most of the early colonies had an official State Religion. They did not enforce conformity but did not take away government-sponsored religion. The Bible was the primary textbook in the public classroom. The early schools were devoted to religious training. Any higher education was under the tutelage of someone at a school dedicated to training ministers, such as at Harvard, Yale, and Princeton.

Different regions had different religious groups that were predominant and, in many ways, favored a certain denomination. They were:

Massachusetts and most of New England: Congregational/Puritan

New York: Dutch Reformed

Rhode Island: Baptist (But open to all)

Pennsylvania: Quaker (But open to all)

Maryland: Catholic

Virginia and the Carolinas: Anglican[280]

---

[280] Britannica Procon. Org. Religion in the Original 13 Colonies https://undergod.procon.org/religion-in-the-original-13-colonies/, Jan 6, 2009, NA, (Accessed Oct. 27, 2024).

This list is a rough rendering of what colonies leaned toward and, in some cases like Virginia, codified as the official religion of the colonies. It was more than the namesake that led to this claim. This observation, evidenced by the colonies' restrictions on other groups, was unfair.

## B. The Struggle for Religious Liberty in all the Colonies

Roger Williams initially came from England to the Massachusetts Bay and Plymouth Colony to preach and serve as a temporary pastor. He upset several leaders and pastors by leading the struggle for early religious liberty. Williams left the Congregational Church and spoke out against any state-sponsored religion. He began a congregation in a new colony of Rhode Island with a free church based on voluntary participation. Some of the Native Americans included in his congregation and mostly in his mission work indicated his sincerity.

Williams was an early Baptist pioneer for religious freedom, having been immersed and espousing Baptist principles of a free church in a free society without government intervention or compulsion favoring a certain denomination. Although looked on as a heretic by the Massachusetts Bay Colony, his ideas ahead of his time made a lot of sense to those who formed the basis for religious liberty in the Constitution after the colonies resounding victory over the British.[281] Working with Williams, John Clarke made Rhode

---

[281] Nelson, *Baptist Biographies and Happenings in American History*, (Faithful Life: Fort, Myers, FL, 2018), 5-8.

Island a haven for religious freedom that allowed faith and practice with no restrictions.

The theological training many of our founding fathers received had a definite bearing on their worldview when it came time to draft the Declaration of Independence. The Continental Congress featured much prayer and Bible Study. The Declaration of Independence featured four direct and subservient statements about God and our dependence on him as a nation. The premise was that our freedoms (which King George had oppressed) were derived from "Nature's God" and endowed by Our Creator, with certain inalienable rights."[282]

Evidence of our founder's influence on the colonies is evident. It made the upcoming war more than a struggle for secular freedom. Still, religious motivation acknowledging our freedoms came from God was in the Declaration, resulting from His protective hand, which is obvious in the document.

## C. The Evolution in the Colonies Toward Religious Liberty in a New Nation.

The wars and struggles throughout Europe over religion led to unholy alliances between church and state. The movement had a strong

---

[282] Dr. David Flick, Christians Heritage Foundation, "The First Prayer in Congress." https://christianheritagefellowship.com/the-first-prayer-in-congress/, Sept 24, 2004, (Accessed October 27, 2024).

religious influence, but the voluntary practice of religion eventually evolved in America. However, religious affiliation was not an option.

Many colonies and later states required those seeking office to strictly follow the Scriptures and a testimony of the candidate's personal faith in Christ. In the early 19th Century, election sermons were a reality in many towns and state capitals. Before elected officials were sworn in, a pastor reminded them of their duties under God through such sermons to which the whole town was invited. The sermons publicly attended addressed the officials as the ones specifically instructed.[283] These practices were not isolated but common throughout New England and towns that looked to God to instruct their political leaders.

## D. Influence on American Revolutionary Leaders

1. Move to a Free Society with Voluntary Religion

The move to a unified nation led many to seek and define the Church's role in society. Steve Farrel highlights John Leland's leadership in getting the First Amendment of the Constitution added to this historic document:

John Leland, a Baptist pastor in Virginia who had stood strong in the face of suppression, lobbied James Madison to adopt a Freedom of Religion

---

[283] Obbie Tyler Todd https://www.obbietylertodd.com/post/a-brief-history-of-the-election-sermon-in-america. Nov 19, 2020, (Accessed October 29, 2024).

amendment protecting churches from discrimination. Leland and the Baptists influenced much of the First Amendment. Religion was given the freedom to be practiced without government interference. The government, in turn, did not sponsor any specific group as a State Religion. God's influence was acknowledged in all aspects of government, and our founding fathers strongly relied on God, as seen in some of our most revered documents. Freedom of Religion was the first freedom mentioned in the Bill of Rights.[284] This freedom is not for Christians to be isolated but to seek to influence the government peacefully, relying on the "Living God."

The Religious Liberty Amendment was approved in part to forbid one group from having their hand on the scale of religious influence. John Leland said, "Truth can take care of itself, needing no civil ruler to steady the ark of God." He concluded, "Government has no more to do with the religious opinions of men than with the principles of mathematics. Let every man speak freely without fear, maintain the principles he believes, worship according to his faith, either one God, three Gods, not God, or twenty Gods: and let government protect Him in so doing."[285] Baptists

---

[284] Steve Farrell ed, "John Leland: Tireless Champion for Religious Liberty", Political Sermons, Founding Era, 1754-1841, John Leland bio, (Accessed October 27, 2024). http://selfeducatedamerican.com/2010/05/02/john-leland-tireless-champion-ofreligious-libertyFeburary 5, 2002, (Accessed April 11, 2018).
[285] Leon McBeth, *The Baptist Heritage* (Broadman: Nashville, 1987), 275.

stood for the freedom of all to practice their faith. It did not mean everyone would agree with them theologically. The preservation of our government and structure depended on His providence, and we as a nation relied on Him and practiced His word while following His leadership.

E. The Constitution and Its Intent of Religious Freedom Religion's Role in Government

The United States became one of the only nations to operate without state-sponsored religion. But this left the churches free to grow and prosper. It left them free to voluntarily affect society without enforcing conformity to any State Religion. This freedom has resulted in some great revivals in our nation and firm reliance on God.

State religion favoring one denomination forbidden in the Constitutional Amendment is the law of the land. The Bill of Rights, with its provision of religious liberty and no favored State Church, had, in effect, sanctioned the Church's denominational concept and ruled out any direct influence of the Church denominations upon the government. Therefore, the denominations were free to define their faith and practices. But what about Christian responsibility for public life and morals? That is where voluntary society came in.[286] Christians were salt and light in the world. They were to influence the government for the good by producing those practicing Christian principles from generation to generation.

---

[286] Shelley, 406

America was a land of many denominations that sprung from the Christian faith and practiced the Judeo-Christian ethic. The root of American law and government comes from this worldview. Any attempt to subvert this worldview and repress the rights of Christians to have a role in government, as some have advocated, is an abridgment of religious liberty and constitutes a violation of our constitutional rights.

We must stand for these freedoms in the face of hostility toward religion and the removal of any references to God the Father and Christ in the public square. It is our fundamental right to express our faith in public and influence society through the driving force of our faith.

There should not be a war between the secular and spiritual in America. One cannot deny the History of Christianity. They also cannot overlook the religious discrimination that existed in some of the major colonies in the first two centuries as a nation. The Constitution calls for a peaceful existence between government and religion, each playing an important role in the nation's history and ongoing operation.

# Chapter 20

# Missionary Movements and More Awakening in America

The result of the Great Awakening was taking the gospel into the world in places people had not heard it before. Now, the power of God through the revival movements was too good to keep in churches and even nations. A spiritually hungry world must look to the true source of truth and have the right relationship with God. The cultural gods and religions in faraway countries did not impede these places from knowing the story of the gospel.

Burdens for the lost people in the world were sincere. It was not the imposing of one culture on another that the world needed. It was the universal message of the gospel meant for the world and birthed in the hearts of those willing to be the first fruits of leading a worldwide missionary effort. William Carey shines as the "Father of Modern Missions" in this regard. His work in India is startling, and how God used Him is an amazing story. Others came beside him in other places to birth a movement that many hoped would continue to grow and produce results worldwide that no one could have thought possible.

# A. The Modern Missionary Movement

## 1. Pietism and its Influence

Pietism was a movement that dealt with the spiritual aspects of Christianity. It emphasizes the deeper life predating Luther and the Reformation. The Moravians were some of the most noted Pietists, and they used their influence to become some of the first missionaries in the 18th century. Count Ludwig Von Zinzendorf (1700-1760) in Germany was one of the leading spokesmen for this movement. He followed Jacob Spener (1635-1727), a preacher who fostered a missionary movement birthed through Pietism.[287] These groups and individuals were forebearers of the modern mission movement. Their biggest takeaway is that they developed a heart for missions and for the world to come to Christ.

One of the greatest sacrifices in Mission History was by two Moravian missionaries. Johann Leonhard Dober and David Nitschmann were two Moravian Brethren who sold themselves into

---

[287] Bainton, Vol. 2, 116

slavery to minister to enslaved people in the West Indies.

In 1732, Dober and Nitschmann felt called to minister to enslaved people on the islands of St. Thomas and St. Croix. When they could not do so, forbidden by the government from going there, they sold themselves to a slave owner and boarded a ship for the West Indies.

The story of Dober and Nitschmann, known as the "Moravian Slaves," is fascinating. It's a popular narrative about Christian missions. The Moravian Church sent missionaries to areas of poverty and spiritual darkness, and these men showed the intensity of their faith to share the gospel with enslaved people, whatever the cost. This most brutal way became a pathway to reach these people for Christ.

The Moravian missionaries were the first large-scale Protestant missionary movement. They were the first to send non-ordained people to the mission field, the first to go to enslaved people, and the first in many countries.[288] Such sacrifice is unheard of in our modern day, but it was a burden God put on their hearts to minister in any way they could. Self-sacrifice was a notable characteristic of the Moravians that became a landmark of the movement.

---

[288] Emancipation of the Freed, NA. https://emancipationofthefreed.blogspot.com/2007/01/john-leonard-dober-and-david-nitschman.html, January 21, 2007, (Accessed November 21, 2024).

In 1727, Zinzendorf was the guiding spirit of Herrnhut (settling the city in Germany as a refuge for Moravians), and ten years later, he received formal ordination in the reorganized Moravian Church, or "United Brethren," as the believers preferred to call it. Zinzendorf influenced these brethren toward missions. His impulses were always strongly missionary. As a result, the Moravians became the first large-scale Protestant missionary force in history to go into needy areas with the gospel.[289] Zinzendorf's influence was primarily in America, but others who followed his passion for reaching the world could provide a good picture of what world missions would be like.

## B. William Carey's Influence

William Carey (1761-1834) was "The Father of Modern Missions." He was a Baptist preacher in England who was a shoe cobbler. Carey studied languages and went to India in 1792 to mark the birth of the Modern Missions Movement. He stayed in India for 43 years and greatly influenced foreign missions. Carey opened the door for missions there and translated the Bible into many languages.[290] This great missionary's influence and courage in going to India is inspirational. He was the first to go to faraway places and cultures that did not understand the Christian message.

Carey was well aware of his predecessors in the great work. As a Baptist pastor in England, Carey became heavily burdened for the

---

[289] Shelley, 347
[290] Meade, 121-122

unevangelized. At a meeting of ministers in Leicester in 1792, he preached a missionary sermon entitled "An Enquiry into the Obligation of Christians to Use Means for the Conversion of the Heathen." Within the famous sermon, he coined his slogan for himself and countless others following him: "Expect Great Things from God, and Attempt Great Things from God."

Later that same year, the Baptist Missionary Society was founded, largely due to Carey's efforts. Carey left for the next year for Bengal, India, as its first missionary. He immersed himself in Bible translation, evangelism, and serving as a pastor.[291] Carey's mastery of translation came from personal study and a lifetime of work in this needful area. This work in itself made his influence very substantial in India. Bingham tracks Carey's progress in missionary efforts in India:

In 1800, Carey moved to Serampore, where he extended his ministry to include Church planting and teaching. Carey did not isolate himself from the larger world. He saw the need to integrate missionary vision into various avenues of life. He worked to provide medical services, produced a Bengali-English dictionary, and founded the Agricultural and Horticultural Society of India. Although the Baptist Missionary Society concentrated its work in India, later, it sponsored work in Jamaica, China, the Cameroons, and the Congo.[292]

---

[291] McBeth,186
[292] Bingham, 154

Carey even got involved in getting the practice of "Sati" abolished. Widow burning had evolved through the ages as a horrible practice. It was a remarkable achievement to abolish this practice. The practice ingrained into the Indian/Hindu culture meant that at a husband's death and cremation, his still-alive wife immediately followed him, being burned with him. You can imagine how this affected many young girls betrothed and married to older men. Carey worked with government representatives to stop this practice and save millions of lives.[293]

The Society founded before Carey left for India had a heart to reach the entire world, so they did not restrict going to places other than India. Shelley explains why Carey was the leader of Foreign Missions going into the 19th Century:

"It was very obvious that William Carey led the charge for Foreign Missions in the new century. Carey thought about the evangelism of whole countries and what happens when whole populations become Christian. He held that the foreign missionary can never make more than a small contribution to accomplishing the work to be done, and that, therefore, the development of the local ministry is the first and greatest of all missionary considerations. Above all, he saw that Christianity must be firmly rooted in the culture and traditions in which it is planted. Carey gained

---

[293] Evangeline Anderson-Rajkumar, Christian History Institute, https://christianhistoryinstitute.org/magazine/article/ministry-in-killing-fields, 1992, (Accessed January, 16, 2025.

the title "Father of Modern Missions" through all these efforts."[294]

Missionaries had not gone as far as Carey had and encountered an antithetical culture, unlike the home he was leaving. He also fostered the way for others to come and serve with him in India and other foreign nations. Carey's encouragement to missions among Baptists was great, according to Shelley:

"Carey's call to action that inspired mission efforts in 1792 awakened many. *An Enquiry into the Obligation of Christians to Use Means for the Conversion of the Heathen* publication was epoch. In it, Carey took up the five objections that people raised against missions to "heathen" lands: their distance, their barbarism, the danger that would be incurred, the difficulties of support, and the unintelligible languages. One by one, he answered these objections. The same obstacles had not prevented the merchants from going to distant shores. "It only requires," he wrote, "that we should have as much love for the souls of our fellow creatures and fellow sinners as they have for the profits arising from a few otter skins, and all these difficulties could be easily surmounted." He ended his appeal with practical proposals for the preaching of the gospel throughout the world."[295]

God had placed the world on Carey's heart and wanted others to join him in His quest,

---

[294] Shelley, 394
[295] Ibid, 395

garnering support for such an endeavor back home.

By encouraging each other, Carey and Andrew Fuller, a pastor and director of the Baptist Mission Society, succeeded in breaking free from the restrictive theology of their time. They went back to the New Testament, especially to Jesus' injunction to preach the gospel to all the world and the apostle Paul's declaration of God's intention: "that at the name of Jesus, every knee should bow, in heaven and on earth and under the earth, and every tongue confess that Jesus Christ is Lord, to the glory of God the Father" (Phil. 2:10, 11). As a result, in October 1792, Carey, Fuller, and eleven Baptist colleagues formed the Baptist Missionary Society, and within a year, Carey and his family were on their way to India.[296] They put their vision and energy into the place where they had a vision. It would be a life-long commitment to hardship and saying goodbye to friends and family, but their heart for the lost in India superseded everything. Others followed Carey to assist him, as Shelley details:

"Later, the East Indian company refused Carey permission to live in Calcutta, so he settled in Serampore under the Danish flag instead. Upon entering India, he secured employment as a foreman of an indigo factory in Bengal. Since the position demanded only three months of the year, he found plenty of time for intensive study of the oriental languages. In 1799, two fellow Baptists,

---

[296] Ibid, 396

Joshua Marshman and William Ward, joined Carey at Serampore. For the next quarter-century, the three men worked together to organize a growing network of mission stations in and beyond Bengal."[297]

Carey's efforts in translation catapulted him there in Serampore. His harsh initial encounter in India reversed to respect gained through his efforts and the translation work that multiplied his work, never to be forgotten.

## C. Adoniram Judson and Luther Rice

Before the American Baptist regional split in 1845, Northern and Southern Baptists sent missionaries to distant places. One tandem of missionaries (Adoniram Judson and Luther Rice) were members of the Congregational Church who sensed God's call to Burma and parts of the Far East. Strongly moved to answer God's call to missions at the Haystack prayer meetings at Williams College, they surrendered to the missionary call. In a further study of the Scriptures, they were convinced immersion was the correct mode of baptism. On their first tour, they stopped in India to discuss believer's baptism with William Carey, who had gone there from England. They were baptized by William Ward in Carey's Lal Bazar Chapel and joined the Baptist Church at Calcutta.

The Congregational Churches sponsored the missionaries, but Judson and Rice asked for sponsorship from the Baptists after their baptism.

---

[297] Ibid

The Baptists gladly accepted them, and they began service under Baptist sponsorship.[298]

Judson had a stellar missionary career in Burma, and Rice became a strong leader in organizing and recruiting others for foreign mission work.

Judson translated *The Grammatical Notices of the Burmese Language,* followed by a translation of the Gospel of Matthew in 1817. He had a passion for translating the Bible into the Burmese language. A printing press arrived from Serampore, India, making their work more available to the population. The new missionary firmly believed in biblical authority and conviction of truth as he worked in Burma.[299]

Judson also endured much suffering on the mission field. A ruler who declared war on all missionaries and foreigners in the country jailed him for being a "suspected spy." He was captured, chained, and hung upside down in a jail. His wife was allowed to visit him, but he was weakened and almost died. He was eventually released, but later, his wife died, and his family suffered much, losing several children to death.[300]

Despite all these difficulties, Judson's translation circulated throughout Burma, and

---

[298] O.K. and Marjorie Armstrong, *The Baptists in America*. (Doubleday: Garden City, NY), 1979, 130.
[299] Courtney Anderson, *To the Golden Shore: The Life of Adoniram Judson*. Judson Press Valley Forge, PA, 1987), 299-300.
[300] Nelson, *Baptist Biographies*, 86-87

today, there is a strong Christian influence in the country. This mission effort became a forerunner for Southern Baptist mission work, which began through Judson and Rice.

Luther Rice had to come back to the States because of physical illness and handicaps. However, he became one of the greatest missionary promoters in the United States. He helped co-found the Triennial Convention dedicated to promoting missions and laid the groundwork for the birth of the Southern Baptist Convention in 1845.[301]

## D. Other Foreign Mission Efforts

In America, Samuel J. Mills (1783-1818) was largely responsible for focusing on foreign missions. In 1810, he and Adoniram Judson (1788-1850) and other students from Andover Seminary helped form the first American foreign missionary society, the American Board of Commissioners for Foreign Missions (ABCFM)—Congregationalist in affiliation. The ABCFM also sponsored missionaries from other denominations.[302] Students' energy and their burden for the world signaled more wonderful challenges met for worldwide missions and gospel expansion.

In the summer of 1806, at Andover Seminary, several students were in prayer at one of their meetings when a thunderstorm forced them to take shelter under a haystack. During this

---

[301] Ibid, 89-91
[302] Bingham, 155

hour of prayer, the group members committed to praying fervently for overseas missions. The "Haystack Prayer Meeting" is frequently highlighted as pivotal in founding American foreign missions.[303] The movement had a small beginning, but the impact was long-lived throughout the new century.

In addition to denominationally sponsored missions, faith missions also arose. These groups were independently founded and were nondenominational or interdenominational. One of these groups was the China Inland Mission (1865), founded by J. Hudson Taylor (1832-1905). Working within the interior of China, Taylor exemplified "becoming Chinese so that he might reach the Chinese." He also practiced full dependence on God and his people for daily and ministerial needs.[302] Hudson Taylor's work was consequential in that others came to support the work and live in the large country that was and still is an important influencer throughout the Far East.

## E. Missionary Awareness at the Turn of the 19th Century

It is no surprise to learn that David Livingstone's (1813-1873) labor in Africa was influenced by his conviction that commerce and Christianity within that country would diminish the slave trade. He arrived under the London Missionary Society in 1840 and died thirty-three years later in modern-day Zambia. As a missionary

---

[303] Ibid, 156

and explorer, he carried out the vision of a devout evangelical member of the British Parliament[304] His journey to the dark continent again paved the way for others to come. His insight as an explorer helped improve people's understanding of Africa. Now, others could give the gospel to those who had never heard it.

Livingstone was a missionary and explorer. Arriving in 1841, Livingstone served for ten years in the ordinary routine of missionary work. But he was not a man to stay long in any one place. The mind and impulse of the explorer were in him, and he was always drawn on, in his own words, by "the smoke of a thousand villages" that had never seen a missionary.[305] This urgency and wonderment drove Livingstone to great exploits. They made him commit to discovering Africa's differences from the rest of the world as he discovered them and revealed them to the world.

William Wilberforce (1759-1833) was the man who led the anti-slavery campaign in England, primarily in the British Parliament. In addition to his duties in Parliament, he was a member of the *Clapham sect*, a group made up of wealthy Anglican evangelicals. Wilberforce and the other members of the sect mobilized against slavery and witnessed the abolition of the slave trade through Britain and its colonies initially in 1807 and ultimately in 1833.[306] Wilberforce was influential in

---

[304] Ibid, 155
[305] Shelley, 398
[306] Ibid

getting slavery removed from England. It took an entire lifetime, but it allowed England to end the practice without firing a shot, an entirely different story from America. This great liberation paved the way for missions to Africa instead of enslaving people.

## F. The Triennial Convention and Cooperation in Missions

The Triennial Convention eventually led to the formation of the Southern Baptist Convention. The Triennial Convention was a missionary group formed by Baptists in America to send out foreign missionaries. The Northern and Southern Baptists split over Churches, sending missionaries with slave owners in them.[307] Missions were a supreme reason for the Southern Baptist Convention's formation. It is seldom realized as its purpose when the split with the Northern Baptists made slavery the big issue.

As mentioned, Luther Rice and Adoniram Judson were missionaries to India and Burma. Rice came back to America to promote the cause of missions. He dreamed of a denomination whose primary purpose was to get the gospel to the whole world. He worked to see this happen but could not bring it to fruition. His dream became reality, though, in 1845, the Southern Baptist Convention was formed in Augusta, Georgia. The Southern Baptist Convention was founded with a desire to take the gospel to everyone in the world, and this

---

[307] Nelson, "William Bullein," Johnson" *Baptist Biographies and Happenings in American History* 97-99.

has been a driving force ever since that time. The split with Northern Baptists did not deter their efforts in World Missions because they did not support Southern Baptist's appointment of various missionaries.[308]

Judson endured hardship in Burma (as mentioned) to translate the Bible into the native language but also blazed a path for others to follow. They could see what impact missionaries could have, as in Judson's case.[309]

Lottie Moon later became the first female missionary under the Southern Baptist Convention, ministering in China and raising missionary awareness in the states to the cause of missions. She was in China for decades and returned after a famine hit the land. She died coming back to the States on a ship. Her example of sacrifice was so great that a missionary offering named after her is collected each Christmas among the Southern Baptist Convention. It is the largest World Missions offering in the world and of all time.[310]

G. The Second Great Awakening Movement and Charles Finney's Leadership

Awakening fires spread in America toward the end of the eighteenth century. These revivals, known as the Second Great Awakening, differed from the First Awakening of the 1740s, particularly in theological emphasis. Geographically, the

---

[308] Ibid, 84-91
[309] Ibid, 89-91
[310] Ibid, 118-119

Second Awakening reached beyond New England to the south and west. It was diverse in character and location. Theologian and Yale president Timothy Dwight (1752-1817) is counted among its proponents, yet Tennessee and Kentucky were among its most flamboyant centers. Revival occurred within universities and also within the camp meetings, and it quickly became the hallmark medium of frontier revivals.[311] As people moved west to different and dangerous places, they took their Christian influence with them. Others came to Christ to cope with the uncertainties of the pioneer area.

The 2nd Great Awakening was generally a movement in the early 1800s in the pioneer states. People experienced a revival as they went westward. Moving west helped expand the gospel message wherever they went.

Charles Finney (1792-1875) was one of New England's most notable preachers in the Awakening movement there. *The Great Prayer Revival* of the late 1850s marked the end of this movement. Finney pioneered many modern revival methods, such as the "come-forward invitation." Great conviction of sin was a notable characteristic of his revivals. Finney's meetings featured a deep conviction of sin, resulting in moral reformation. He was Arminian in theology and emphasized strongly

---

[311] Bingham, 144

the free will of man. Many emotional excesses carried over from this movement until today.[312]

Finney's impact in New England is vast. Though some disagreed with his theology and methods, whole towns were impacted by the meetings he conducted there. Bingham's alerts to the difference Finney has from the leaders of the First Great Awakening:

"There was a difference in Theology from the First Great Awakening during the Second Great Awakening. Theologically, while the First Awakening had maintained a strong Calvinistic heritage, the Second was more sympathetic to an Arminian tone. Traced back to Jacob Arminius (1605-1690), Arminianism was a movement within the Dutch Reformed Church that rejected the Calvinistic emphases on predestination and irresistible grace. According to Arminianism, God provides prevenient grace, which enables the fallen human will to respond freely to grace. The human will can freely cooperate with grace and believe or freely refuse to cooperate and not believe. Calvinism, however, emphasized salvation as entirely an act of God from start to finish. The elect will believe because God foreordained it. In Arminianism, receiving grace is conditional on people's free response, but in Calvinism, God's grace is irresistible."[313]

---

[312] Who was Charles Finney?, (https://www.gotquestions.org/Charles-Finney.html), NA, ND), (Accessed Nov 4, 2024).
[313] Bingham,144

Many Christians believe in one of these two differences in theology. God can use different theological views for his glory if they get the gospel out to people.

For the Second Great Awakening, Charles G. Finney (who was both one of its products and one of its representatives) thought revival was largely an issue of method, tactic, and technique. The evangelists employed strategies aimed at developing an atmosphere of dramatic conversions. The camp meetings in the frontier areas provided such an environment. The meetings, held in areas remote from towns or cities, featured hundreds of people confined in close quarters for several days, listening to repetitive gospel messages and appeals for decisions.[314] New methods like city-wide meetings and going into places where churches did not exist popularized the gospel. Bingham goes on to describe Finney's theology, which was different from most orthodox groups, particularly leaning toward Calvinism:

"Finney believed everyone was reachable for Christ. His methods were strongly linked to his theology. For Finney, a revival was not a miracle, for nothing in religion lay beyond ordinary laws of nature. Humans who became spiritually alive were not supernaturally enabled to become something they had been unable to be before. Revival was simply humans freely using natural powers in ways that glorified God. Therefore, he believed that

---

[314] Ibid, 145

**235**

revival could be brought about through proper use of means. Finney argued in favor of these natural means to revival in his 1835 lectures in New York City and published them under the title *Lectures on Revivals of Religion*. He defined revival as "a purely philosophical result of the right use of the constituted means – as much so as any other effect produced by the application of means."[315]

Finney believed God could bring revival through those who prepared their hearts and worked to see it happen. Finney's views on conversion again differed from traditional emphasis up to his leadership, according to Bingham:

"Finney taught that conversion is something people are totally capable of doing themselves. In a sermon preached in 1835, "Sinners Bound to Change Their Own Hearts," he set forth the following theses from Ezekiel 18:31, which contains the phrase "get a new heart and a new spirit." We have the powers of moral agency . . . We do not need to be altered in soul or body; we do not need to add to our minds any new principle . . . The new heart and spirit are not constitutional changes in our human nature. The change of heart Ezekiel spoke of is not miraculous; it is just a choice we make to employ our abilities in obedience to God rather than in self-gratification."[316]

No human effort can bring salvation, but Finney believed revival was God-honoring people's hard work to make it happen. Finney's supposed

---

[315] Ibid,
[316] Bingham, 146

belief in the atonement is surprising as Bingham uncovers:

Against this background of free moral agency and denial of human bondage to sin, Finney's view of the atonement also differed from that of the leaders of the First Awakening. He did not preach the crucifixion of Christ as a penal substitutionary atonement. That is, Christ did not suffer in our place as our substitute, bearing on himself our punishment. Rather, Finney preached what is called a governmental and moral influence view of the atonement. In his sermon "On the Atonement" he announced that Christ "was not punished." Christ's death made a governmental statement. It testified to God's high regard for the law, which had been broken by sin, and his hatred for sin. At the cross, God gave "a demonstration of His attitude toward sin."[317]

This portion of Finney's theology is opposed justly. Clarity about the sacrifice of Christ for our sin needs more understanding by those who studied his theology and did not discover it.

The work of the Second Great Awakening was not as lasting as the First Great Awakening in the 18th Century regarding denominations and societies being formed. The emotional excesses associated with these meetings were a primary reason for the Awakening continuing under other leaders. In the latter part of the 19th Century, under Spurgeon and Moody, the revivals of note featured a direct emphasis on the Bible and

---

[317] Ibid

preaching God's Word as preeminent in these meetings.

Whole denominations formed for foreign missions demonstrate God's desire for those who never heard the gospel to listen and respond to it. The needy world will not wait for God's burden on hearts unless that sense of urgency exists.

As the Second Great Awakening spread in America, a new breath of fresh air inspired others. They pledged to go far away and give their lives for the cause of Christ and the mission He had placed on their hearts. It is an amazing story that should never be forgotten.

# Chapter 21

# Evangelical Influences in the 19th Century

The Evangelical movement of the 19th century was the springboard for great revival led by memorable preachers. Spurgeon's role as a Reformed Baptist preacher was secondary to his excellent preaching and the growth the Metropolitan Tabernacle experienced under his leadership. William Booth's Methodist affiliation was secondary to his working with the poor and desolate on the streets of London. These great ministries influenced people and still do so today.

The Civil War featured a reliance on God in battle and as a nation on both sides, even while 600,00 were slaughtered in battle. Some would say seeing God's will amid such carnage is inconsistent. However, Lincoln included God's guidance in much of his writing and speeches (particularly) The Gettysburg Address. The terrible war got people thinking about how useless much of the carnage was, and they looked to God for healing and help.

The 19th century closed with an evangelist for the everyday person. D.L. Moody conducted massive crusades and saw many coming to Christ. His example of personal witnessing still indicates how he was a common man God used for a common purpose.

All these leaders and movements featured a progressive movement toward the agreement of getting out the gospel to people regardless of their denomination. For this reason, God did great things through these influences in the 19th Century.

# A. Charles Spurgeon's Role in English Christianity

Charles Spurgeon (1834-1892) was a famous Baptist preacher in London who preached to crowds of over 12,000 a Sunday. He was a notable expository preacher who preached through the Bible. His sermons sparked mission movements and great exploits. Spurgeon was a committed Calvinist but saw many trust in Christ during his ministry. He defended Biblical Christianity from liberalism in the "Downgrade controversy" toward the latter end of his ministry. His sermons are still read and studied today.[318] All his sermons preserved gave a good window into the topics and doctrinal understandings of the Scripture. His

---

[318] David Beale, *Baptist History in England and America: Personalities, Positions, and Practices.*
(Xulon Press: Maitland, FL, 2018), 331.

passion for communicating and burden for souls saw his sermons and ministry rise to worldwide significance.

# B. William Booth and the Salvation Army

William Booth (1829-1912) founded the Salvation Army. He came out of the Methodist movement and had a deep burden for the slums of London and the poverty-stricken people there. He gave birth to a sacrificial group of people deeply devoted to helping others experiencing poverty.[319] The army became a vanguard for help to those in desperate conditions. His ministry reached the down and out and continues to this day.

William Booth started the ministry of the Salvation Army with the *Methodist New Connection* but soon withdrew to work with London's poor. His street preaching in London's East End in 1864 met with phenomenal success. Within eleven years, he had thirty-two stations promoting evangelism and social service among London's destitute. His workers, organized like a military unit, were soon called the Salvation Army. Evangelist Booth became General Booth.[320] The discipline his troops marched under was impressive. They made a supernatural effort to reach those needing the love of Christ badly.

By 1888, the General had established 1,000 British Corps and had dispatched patrols to many

---

[319] Bainton vol. 2, 156
[320] Shelley, 432

other nations. His book *In Darkest England and the Way Out* appeared in 1890 and graphically compared the social darkness in England to Africa's darkness, as pictured by David Livingstone.[321] Meeting physical needs led to spiritual needs with which they shared the gospel. The impact of such a ministry is worldwide.

# C. The Civil War

The Civil War was a horror for the United States but amid all the death and carnage, some spots led people to look to the Lord. In Lincoln's Second Inaugural Address – he observed: "Both the Union and Confederacy read the same Bible, and pray to the same God, and each invokes his aid against the other. . . The prayers of both cannot be answered. . . The Almighty has his own purposes." Lincoln knew that men should try to do God's will as well as they could determine what it was for them, but the Almighty has His purposes that go beyond the plans of men.[322] Deep soul-searching was evident as thousands were dying around them. The small items were insignificant to the eternal ramifications of those dying in battle. Death was the great equalizer of both sides. Shelley describes the role Harriet Beecher Stowe had in stoking the fires for the Civil War:

"Others tried to figure out where God was in all the fighting and death. Harriet Beecher Stowe wrote the national epic *Uncle Tom's Cabin*. She was striking at the national conscience in the hope that

---

[321] Ibid
[322] Ibid, 412

a cleansing of the nation's soul would avert a divine scourging of the body politic. All sides in the struggle used the same set of symbols. There was one Bible, one Heaven, one Hell, one Jesus Christ, and one path of salvation. Yet the symbols were employed for opposite causes. How could God be the God of the South against the North and the North against the South? How could He have sponsored slavery, as Southerners said, and opposed slavery, as Northerners contended?"[323]

Slavery was the issue that made a growing and prospering nation stop in its tracks. The questions, unfortunately, people had been answered by blood in the war. The country did heal eventually after such a life sacrifice. Questions continued when Lincoln's assassination evoked such sorrow and regret. Yet, peace eventually came to a nation divided but now one again.

## D. The Moody Phenomena

D.L. Moody (1837-1899) was a famous evangelist who started a great Church and school in Chicago. He popularized evangelism methods such as crusades and personal soul-winning. He had a tremendous burden for souls and was used mightily with limited education.[324] Moody's passion to reach people everywhere was the secret of his successful ministry. He had a burden for the lost,

---

[323] Ibid, 411

[324] David Mass, "The Life and Times of D.L. Moody," https://christianhistoryinstitute.org/magazine/article/life-and-times-of-moody, Christian History, Issue 25, 1990. (Accessed, Dec. 4, 2024,}

leading him to constantly talk to people about the gospel.

Moody became the major urban revivalist during the last half of the nineteenth century following the Civil War. D. L. Moody and scores of lesser-known preachers felt their primary task was winning souls to Christ and preparing saved men and women for Christ's second coming.[325] God's hand was upon him, as witnessed by many who listened and came to Christ through his extensive attempts to share Christ daily. He set the example of how massively God can use someone committed to His purpose in their life.

The door was now open through this massive movement under Moody to see the gospel preached in a new and modern century. This new century would still carry with it the movements of the past century that God had used so mightily. The fact that these men are still quoted and memorialized in our time points to their continuing influence and ministry remembered to the present day.

One is not likely to forget the mark these men made on the world for being available to God and His work through them. The results of what God accomplished through them is still desired today and duplicated as they sent their legacy into the new century. Their influence, not forgotten, is emulated by many to the present day.

---

[325] Ibid, 413-414

# Chapter 22

# The Rise of Major Cults in the 19th Century

Opposition developed as the gospel went out through false movements and famous leaders through their influence. These movements were contrary to the gospel and the special way God blessed the evangelistic and missionary movements of the 19th century.

Despite great revival and missionary movements in the 19th century, it featured the rise of three distinctively American cults that reared up against the tide of God's spirit moving. The State Church advocates would say it was because of absolute religious liberty that allowed cults to thrive. The more perceptive observer would say that the cults arose because of the counterfeit that Satan always has for God's truth (Rom 1:23 a).

As God was working in the 2nd Great Awakening, Spurgeon, and Moody revivals, Satan was trying to supplant what God was doing through these counterfeit movements. They are still with us today and have given rise to other cults that have some of their features. Three main cults started in the 19th Century.

## A. Jehovah's Witnesses

Charles Taze Russell (1852-1917) founded Jehovah's Witnesses after the Civil War. Noted for their denial of the Trinity and the Deity of Christ, His atonement and bodily resurrection, and eternal torment, while setting dates for the battle of Armageddon, marking the end of the world, they oppose all other groups, believing they are the only ones right. Jehovah's Witnesses are conscientious objectors who oppose the government and defense of the country.[326] Much of what the Witnesses expounded and practiced made them social dropouts. Yet, they grew through Scripture twisting and trying to get their message to the world.

Jehovah Witnesses kept evolving into the 20th century. Judge J. F. Rutherford (1869-1942), at the turn of the century, became the leader of the Jehovah's Witnesses. Until 1935, you could be one of the 144,000 in heaven, but now you will only reign on earth after joining their group. This change is because

---

[326] Walter Martin, "Jehovah's Witnesses and the Watchtower Bible and Tract Society" *The Kingdom of the Cults*, 2003) 69-83.

they exceeded 144,000, now reserved for those in their group truly worthy because of their service. They feature a heavy works salvation and encouragement of everyone to go door to door and make converts to their group.[327] The works salvation they espoused led to others joining and working for salvation to what they thought was awaiting them.

Jehovah's Witnesses are very millennial-oriented in their feeling that the end of the world is coming soon with the battle of Armageddon taking place. In their last times teaching, the world is incinerated, and they will be the only ones left to rule and reign in Jehovah's theocratic kingdom. They used to predict that Jesus would come visibly but have changed their view, thinking that Jesus came invisibly in 1917 and is ruling through them as they establish His kingdom on earth.

Jehovah's Witnesses are a remake of the Gnostic and Arian controversy in that they believe Jesus was a created individual who was not God but lower than God, who to them is only Jehovah. They do not celebrate Christmas because of its association with the worship of Christ. They believe Jesus was Michael the archangel and certainly not the God-man.

Jehovah's Witnesses do not believe Jesus died for sin. They feel He was put to death on a torture stake and killed as an example of God's love. They don't believe Jesus was raised bodily. They feel his manifestations after the resurrection were only a spirit inspiring faith in the disciples.

---

[327] Alan Street, Cult Invasion, Street Meetings: Dallas, 1989), NP.

Jehovah's Witnesses do not believe in a literal Hell that has eternal fire. They think that Hell only means the grave. God may burn up people after the battle of Armageddon but will not do it eternally, according to them.[328]

All of these beliefs are outside the range of Christians who believe in the gospel as believed since the time of Christ. A works salvation and denial of the person and work of Christ put them in opposition to orthodoxy and in a category they have chosen for themselves.

Jehovah's Witnesses are very works-oriented, believing they earn a place in God's kingdom by winning converts to their group. They go door to door selling literature and trying to enroll people in a seven-step program that begins with Bible Study from the book *The Truth that Leads to Eternal Life*. The witnesses' step-by-step instructions have landed many unknowing and unsuspecting people in their organization.

Headquartered in Brooklyn, New York, they are a hierarchical group that hands down doctrine from those headquarters. They believe the Watchtower Bible and Tract Society is a prophetic organization, and they said so in an April 1972 publication.[329] The top-heavy revelations given by the Watchtower have

---

[328] Ibid, Martin and Street

[329] (Quora,https://www.quora.com/Why-did-the-Watchtower-Organization-claim-to-be-a-prophet-of-God-in-Apr-1-1972-p-197-WT-since-they-have-changed-many-understandings-such-as-the-generation-in-the-time-of-the-end-claiming-it-is-light-from-God), ND., NA. (Accessed October 28, 2024).

left the members of the group dependent on them for whatever way the wind is blowing when it comes to changes in their prophecy, theology, and methods.

Although Jehovah's Witnesses are social dropouts, they have always been aggressive in seeking converts for their group. Because of their aggressive nature, they have grown into a large movement through their works-oriented teaching one has to do to accomplish salvation. It may not be wise to use the witnesses as an example for witnessing and being outward in our faith. Their gospel is different from any other group by design and to their eventual demise.

# B. Mormonism

The Church of Jesus Christ of Latter-Day Saints (The Mormons) was founded by Joseph Smith (1805-1844). He said he had found an additional revelation to the Bible in the *Book of Mormon*. He was said to have translated it but enlisted Sidney Rigdon, an associate of Solomon Spaulding (a local author in New York State), who forged Spaulding's work called *Manuscript Found* into Smith's book. The book features how the Native Americans came to this country, the history of their people here, and their wars. Some of these stories are pure speculation. Smith said his translation of the *Book of Mormon* came from golden plates; the angel Maroni told him to dig them up at a certain place. The prospects of this discovery happening at a certain location are impossible.[330] Many holes are in the account of Smith's discovery and initiation of the Latter-Day Saints.

Smith said God told him not to join any religion but to restore the true Church of Jesus Christ. Everywhere Smith moved, those who revealed his fraud would follow him, necessitating his followers to be continually on the move. His followers continued to move west, where he was captured, and a mob killed him in Nauvoo, Illinois, while he was in jail. Before Smith died, he had begun the practice of polygamy among his followers, taking several wives himself. [331] Polygamy was not taught as normal in the Scripture and not as an example in the New Testament. Smith's ability to switch ideas on a dime was truly amazing. Many have said his demise was unfortunate for the chance of his group running amuck and dying if he continued to live. Smith's continual revelations and changes would have eventually killed his "new religion."

Smith's Mormon successor, Brigham Young, helped carve an empire in the West with what became the state of Utah. Mormons believe in plural marriages, polytheism, and denial of Christ's deity, His virgin birth, and His atoning sacrifice. They believe Christ reappeared to the Native Americans in America, and the *Book of Mormon* is a record of this

---

[330] Wayne Cowdrey, Howard A. Davis & Donald R. Scales *Who Really Wrote the Book of Mormon?* (Vision House: Santa Ana, CA, 1977) 94-104.
[331] Frank Barnes, "Ten False Teachings of Mormonism" Church Membership Orientation for Baptist Churches, (The Shop at Arpop: Longview, Texas, 1975), 1-2.

allegedly happening and as an additional revelation to Scripture. They also feature heavy works-salvation and a strong missionary force designed to proselyte others into their group. The aim is to get to the third heaven. They do not believe in Hell.

There is an assortment of other religions that influenced Mormonism. Baptismal Regeneration-Church of Christ, Priesthood-Catholicism, Tongues-Charismatic movement, Secret Rites –Freemasonry, Baptism for the Dead and Spirit Beings-Spiritism.[332] The restricting of what they believed Jesus came to do and the extra-biblical beliefs make the Saints a cult, again fully outside the mainstream of orthodox beliefs shared by Bible-believing Christians.

When Utah wanted admittance as a state, the United States government said they would have to abandon polygamy. They instead told the government they could not since it was a part of their religion. When threatened with marital law, the 12 Apostles who succeeded Young said, "God told them polygamy was only to be practiced in heaven." This change brings up an interesting point about Mormons.[333] Changing different beliefs to accommodate the culture or, for a specific reason, needing to change is troubling.

---

[332]Walter Martin, The Maze of Mormonism, Vison House: Santa Ana, California, 1962,106-130

[333] The Manifesto and the End of Plural Marriage" NA, https://www.Churchofjesuschrist.org/study/manual/gospel-topics-essays/the-manifesto-and-the-end-of-plural-marriage?Lang=eng, ND, (Accessed October 29, 2024

Mormons believe in continuing revelation, as in the late 1970s, when they changed their view on black's admittance to the priesthood. Continuing revelation seems to be whatever is most politically expedient at the time.[334] The willingness to change through continued revelation shows how Mormons seek to blend into the culture, and although they have exclusive beliefs, they want acceptance as a legitimate "Christian group."

Continuing revelation is the Mormon's reason for believing the *Book of Mormon* is another testament to Christ of equal and of higher value than the Bible. They say the Bible is correct only when "correctly translated." This doctrine means that its teachings do not contradict the *Book of Mormon*. Given this new revelation, they believe they are The Restored Church of Christ of Latter Day Saints.[335] *The Book of Mormon* seems to be more revered than the Bible. The equal adoration of it with the Bible shows how continued revelation moved them to not believe in the closed canon of Scripture.

Mormonism also believes in other revelations such as *The Pearl of Great Price*, *Doctrine and Covenants*, and the teachings of Smith and Young.[336] The reference to their founders shows

---

[334] The Church of Jesus Christ study manual, (https://www.Churchofjesuschrist.org/study/manual/gospel -topics-essays/race-and-the-priesthood?lang=eng), NA, ND, (Accessed October 29, 2024) 64

[335] John Smith, *Witnessing Effectively to Mormons*,: (Utah Missions: Marlowe, OK, 1975), 64.

[336] Ibid, 65-66

how they accept these other documents as legitimate and equal to the Scripture.

Mormons' view of Christ is really strange. They believe He was the spirit brother of the devil, a product of sexual relations between Adam and Mary. He was a polygamist who had children from Mary and Martha, which he saw when he died on the cross.[337] These teachings have led many to exclaim that the Mormons don't believe everything their group has espoused since it is so way out of touch with Biblical Orthodoxy.

Another strange teaching by the Mormons is Jesus was a man who became a god, just like us, so that we can become a god. A statement of theirs is: "As man is so God once was, and as God is, man may become." So, God is an exalted man who has lived in heaven and procreates other little gods. The devout Mormon is trying to achieve godhood and the 3rd heaven since they do not believe in Hell. They achieve godhood through good works and abstaining from alcohol, tobacco, and caffeine.[338] These practices possibly appeal to those who want a clean-cut model of what people may think Christianity is all about. However, these are not the main teachings of Christianity. They are walking testimonies through their commitment to further the Church's expansion of their belief in these false teachings.

---

[337] Barnes, Frank, The *False Teachings of Mormonism, Church Membership Orientation for Baptist Churches*), 5.
[338] Richard Abanes, *Becoming Gods*. Harvest House: Eugene, OR, 179-181.

Mormonism is a vast empire today with many economic investments that have made them rich. They boast the world's largest mission force among youth since each committed youth is required to serve on a mission for two years to prove their sincerity and start on their path to godhood. Unlike Jehovah's Witnesses, Mormons get involved in the community since they demonstrate patriotism and a strong moral life. They continue to expand as they aggressively seek converts.[339]

# C. Christian Science

Christian Science was founded by Mary Baker Eddy (1821-1910). She sought to exalt the mind over matter by healing sickness and denying pain and suffering. God is a force, not a person, in this movement.[340] The group appeals to the spiritual and belief in a faith based on overcoming circumstances and physical obstacles in this life.

Christian Science denies sin, sickness, and death. Biblical revelation is obsolete to this group. They deny every aspect of Jesus' ministry: His virgin birth, death, and resurrection. Metaphysical teaching becomes an avenue to victory over our existence here. Mrs. Eddy's teachings are viewed on the same level as the Bible. Much of her teachings are the basis for New-Age religions. Other groups, such as Unity and Religious Science,

---

[339] Author's observation in his knowledge of them, serving as a pastor with a heavy Mormon population and in conversation with missionaries.
[340] Martin, 38-39

have risen out of this group.[341] The beliefs and practices of these groups have modernized Christian Science.

Mrs. Eddy was from Boston, where the mother Church of Christian Science began. She was in a liberal area that had moved from a haven for strong biblical teaching under the Puritans to an area affected by Unitarianism and Universalism by the 19th Century. The area had much of an influence on who she was and what she was seeking to accomplish.[342] The move away from orthodox Christian beliefs has resulted in what Eddie offered in her teachings.

Eddy's quest was much like Pietism in that they were tired of all the infighting among state churches over doctrinal matters. However, whereas the Pietists were driven to the Scripture to follow Christ more devotedly, they emphasized how they lived over doctrinal fine points they fought over, but it was not so with Eddy. She boldly rejected all the creeds and confessions of the Church and established her own Jesus to fit her sentimentality and experience. The result was a violent rejection of all the cardinal doctrines of Christianity and a diversion to another Jesus that had nothing to do with the Bible.

Eddy's contorted understanding of the Bible became the norm of teaching. In any Christian Science Church, there will be reading (usually from the Bible) on one side of the platform and

---

[341] Ibid, 162-167
[342] Ibid, 157

commentary from her work *Science and Health with Key to Scriptures* to the passage of the Bible study on the other side.[343]

The elevation of Eddy in the Church she left behind again emphasizes the founder instead of biblical authority. This observation is especially true since her teaching contradicts the Scriptures as originally given and believed through the centuries.

Eddy believed in mind over manner as the secret of healing all diseases. She testified to her healing this way, with God saving her life for a divine purpose. Christian Science has practitioners who pray for the illness of members but discourage their followers from going to the doctor. They have no trust in the medical profession or physicians. They become their own physicians through their faith.[344] This rejection of medical doctors makes Christian Science a social outcast in the same way the other cults have proven to exhibit. The fact that Christian Science has declined illustrates how a group built on a personality generally does not

---

[343] Christian Science, Online Sunday Church Service, https://www.christianscience.com/publications-and-activities/online-services-and-events/online-sunday-Church-service Christian Science Online Worship Service, https://www.christianscience.com/publications-and-activities/online-services-and-events/online-sunday-Church-service, ND, NA, (Accessed October 29, 2024).
[344] Christian Science Online Worship Service, https://www.christianscience.com/publications-and-activities/online-services-and-events/online-sunday-Church-service, ND, NA, (Accessed October 29, 2024).

perpetuate the movement started by a person and not God.

Today, Christian Science, unlike Jehovah's Witnesses and Mormonism, is dwindling and not growing in number, with only a handful of people in their churches. But the real impact on Christian Science has been the mindset it has created to doubt God's Word as given for our final authority, creating another Jesus, minimizing sin, making it relative, and the feeling we are our own salvation if we will only have enough faith. Given these radical beliefs, Christian Science is neither Christian nor Science. But the mindset of Christian Science is prevalent throughout our society and finds willing adherents to think in such a way that denies the Scripture and puts eternal souls in peril.[345] Any attempt to change the Bible or deny it defines any group as a cult when it comes to Christianity and its basic truths.

The cults teach us that where biblical truth is alive and active, there will always be a substitute to lead people falsely away from the truth. However, we may know deception is alive to us as believers. These groups still survive today as a substitute for the real thing when it comes to Christian beliefs and practices, evidenced by their influence on people. It is good to know what the cults believe so that they can trap no one. Their history illustrates man-made beginnings despite their gains, even today.

---

[345] Martin, 130-132

These cults were birthed and thrived in the 19th century. The diversion of biblical truth was active and still is in our day. The departure from Biblical Christianity was a noticeable feature of these groups, presenting a difficulty in using the Bible as an authority in dealing with them. Understanding their origins, however, helps us witness and give them the truth of God's Word.

A person can be lost in false religion as they can with no religion at all. False religion muddies the water so that one cannot understand the clear message of the gospel. All the false information and worship turning from the true and living God with His message in the Bible is falsehood. This false information makes it useless to stick one's head in the sand when approaching these movements. Instead, it is good to be well-informed and ready to give an answer for the hope within us (I Pet. 3:15).

## Chapter 23

# Challenges to Christianity in the 20th Century

The entry into the 20th Century brought new challenges to Christianity by discovering new ways that made life easier and more developed than the previous time. There were challenges in the 19th century that continued into the 20th century in religion and the secular realm. Discoveries and theories brought some of their truths into sharp contact with Christianity. Contrasts drawn and differences expanded perpetuated the disagreements. Modern man, who approached learning and inquiry from a secular perspective, looked at the truths of Christianity as part of the past, and many cried for a move beyond the Bible's teachings and a Christian message.

Instead of God being our authority and His Word as a pathway for living, man found himself left to his own devices. In a rational world, he was logical in his approach to discoveries and dismissed Christianity as irrational. This dismissal was even though many truths of Scripture cannot be approached rationally but through faith. So, instead of understanding to believe, we believe to know about God, His Word, and our faith to understand.

## A.  Evolution and Modern Science

The argument over evolution taught in school broke out in Dayton, Tennessee. The Scopes trial in 1925 featured the debate over different views of the Origins of Life. Charles Darwin's *Origin of the Species* made many believe that Science and the Bible were incompatible. Recent studies have proven much evidence for creationism. God did create man, and much of modern science verified through Scripture is a reality (Isaiah 40:22)."[346] Darwin's theory was welcomed by those who did not want to accept the Bible and its teachings. Bingham describes the history of the Scopes trial, which was the flash point for the role of evolution in education:

"The Scopes Trial symbolized the conflict between evolution and the Bible in America. John T. Scopes, accused of breaking Tennessee law by teaching evolution, challenged traditional teaching.

---

[346] Colin Brown, Tim Dowley ed, "Fredrick Schleiermacher," *The History of Christianity*, (Lion Publishers: Oxford, England: 1977), 551.

Clarence Darrow, a religious skeptic, headed his defense, and the fundamentalists placed their hopes for the prosecution in William Jennings Bryan. Although Scopes was found guilty, a verdict later overturned his case by a higher court on a technicality, with fundamentalism receiving ridicule. To many in America, both modernist and fundamentalist, it appeared that the fundamentalists had lost the day – and their once-respected place in culture. They were now on the defensive."[347]

A war was declared on religious views of creation and the Bible, although many still believed. The elites tried to dominate the information related to Darwin's theory. Yet, Churches would not let the theory lie innocent and taught to impressable children. Shelley gives a History of Evolution and how Darwin and his views gained popularity:

Evolution had been around since the 1800's. Darwin's theory was new but popular among many scientists and critics of the Bible. In 1859, Darwin's views appeared in his *Origin of Species*. He contended "that species have been modified during a long course of descent chiefly through the normal selection of numerous successive, slight, favorable variations. The *Origin of Species*, viewed by many as the most important book of the century, revolutionized the concepts about the origin and evolution of life on planet Earth. Darwin followed his first bombshell with a second. In 1871, his

---

[347] Bingham, 163

*Descent of Man* applied natural selection to human beings and reached the controversial conclusion that man's ancestors were probably monkey-like animals.[348]

Darwin's second book created the controversy. Now, those who believed in the Bible that man made in the image of God were under attack.

# B.  Liberalism

Liberalism called for the outright denial of basic truths central to Bible-believing Christians. It questioned the Bible's authenticity and literal use in a changing culture. Liberalism was popularized by Harry Emerson Fosdick and became particularly prevalent in mainline denominations affiliated with the World Council of Churches and liberal seminaries. Liberalism starts with a denial of biblical authority and features a symbolic interpretation of Scripture. It deemphasizes the "New Birth" and tries to make Christianity accommodating to science. This conclusion has led to "Theistic Evolution" and "Neo-Orthodoxy". It is a parasite to a church or denomination. It does not give life but sucks it out of spiritually alive churches.[349] This statement was proven by the decline of liberal denominations and churches that used to be strong in communities or regions. If the Bible is not trustworthy, the assumption is that the Church cannot be trusted either.

---

[348] Shelley, 418
[349] Latourette vol. 2, 1420

Influential pastors joined the chorus of critics of a literal interpretation of the Bible. Henry Ward Beecher (1813-1887), a pastor in Brooklyn, said that the old story just wouldn't do. In a lecture at Yale University in 1872, he argued that the intellectual sophistication of the modern world could no longer accept the ancient doctrines.[350] This statement shocked conservative Christians and churches who had been in the majority.

Liberalism did not give much hope to anyone since its critical nature had lashed out against the traditional interpretation of Scripture. No one expressed the irony of liberalism better than H. Richard Nyberg when he said, "In liberalism, a God without wrath brought men without sin into a kingdom without judgment through the ministrations of a Christ without a Cross."[351] These denials of basic truths taught in the Bible left any church or denomination hopeless and helpless to continue to minister in a church and with the Bible.

Others rejoiced in the progressive nature of liberalism. Henry Sloane Coffin at New York's Union Seminary once said, "Liberalism is that spirit that reveres truth supremely and, therefore, craves the freedom to discuss, publish, and pursue what it believes to be true."[352] However, foundational truths one believes true in liberalism are subject to the scrutiny of the Bible and those who have declared its basic message through the ages.

---

[350] Bingham,153
[351] Shelley, 416
[352] Ibid,

There was a certain elitism that pervaded the liberal camp. Kenneth Couther said that the evangelical liberals were "serious Christians" – to borrow Fosdick's terms – who were searching for a theology that could serve "intelligent moderns."[353] This statement in itself was a snobbery aimed at Christians who defended the literal interpretation of the Bible and stood for its basic teachings as was believed through the ages. Shelley explains the new way liberalism stressed biblical interpretation:

"The new interpreters of Scripture felt they were doing God and the Church service a favor through their criticism of the Bible. The lower critics of the Bible dealt with problems of the text and tried to weigh the merits of many manuscripts of the Bible to find the earliest and most reliable text of Scripture. Higher criticism, however, proved another matter; the higher critic is not primarily interested in the accuracy of the text; he is interested in the meaning of the words. He wants to read between the lines and get behind the text to the events as they really happened. To do so, he must find out when each passage of Scripture was written, who wrote it, and to whom and why it was written. The higher critic believes we can only understand the Bible if we see it against its background."[354]

These methods of biblical criticism pervaded the liberal camp. The liberal approaches the Scripture with unbelief and looks to disassemble

---

[353] Ibid
[354] Ibid, 419

the truth. The Conservative scholar starts from faith and looks to the Lord for guidance and God's message in the passage. These big differences divide the liberal and conservative camps regarding biblical interpretation.

Now imposed on churches and denominations, a new method of discerning truth came into vogue. When liberals could no longer rest in the traditional doctrines of orthodoxy – which they felt science and history had destroyed – they found their needed assurance in the other pillar of their bridge: the "Christian experience."[355] Existentialism added private experience as more important than biblical truth. The truth now believed through one's personal experience became acceptable and a standard for faith.

## C.  The Social Gospel

The Social Gospel is liberalism's counterpart to evangelism. Fredrick Schleiermacher pioneered this movement, which featured helping people with their physical needs and ignoring their spiritual ones.[356] It has taken many churches away from Biblical Christianity. Spiritual needs took a back seat to physical ones, which sounded noble but loaded with problems.

Ministry to the physical took the emphasis off the spiritual. Fredrick Schleiermacher said that orthodox Christians had identified religion with

---

[355] Ibid, 421
[356] Colin Brown, Fredrich Schleiermacher "the History of Christianity, 549

creeds, and men who could no longer accept the creeds thought they were through with religion. But this was a tragic mistake, for they still were in contact with God through their feeling of dependence upon the universe.[357] He was calling those who had given up on basic Christianity as it had been believed and practiced through the ages to see the Christian ethic of helping their fellow man, although they denied its teachings. It was the Christian ethic he was after and taught regardless of one's beliefs.

Sin occurs, says Schleiermacher, when man tries to live by himself, isolated from the universe and his fellow men. He lives for his selfish interest but finds himself miserable.[358] The Christian ethic demands helping our fellow man, which sounded good on the surface. We get the term "the brotherhood of man," as Schleiermacher taught. Service to our fellow man was more important than Scripture. Yet, it is from the Scripture that we fully believe we get the Christian ethic.

Doctrine was not the answer for Schleiermacher. To overcome the sin that separates man from God and man from his fellow man, God sent a mediator in Jesus Christ. Schleiermacher says Christ's uniqueness is not in some doctrine about Jesus or some miraculous origin, such as the Virgin Birth. The real miracle is Jesus himself. In Jesus, we find a man with a

---

[357] Shelley, 422
[358] Ibid

supreme degree of God-consciousness.[359] In stating his view of Jesus, Schleiermacher revealed his hand. You could believe whatever you want to about Jesus as long as one ministered to his fellow man and his needs.

Since Jesus has complete knowledge of God, He can communicate the consciousness of God to others. In Schleiermacher, the center of religion shifted from the Bible to the believer's experience.[360] Schleiermacher advocated existent-ialism, as did liberalism, which made one's belief (even if opposed to the Scripture) the mainstay of faith and practice.

Schleiermacher was "the father of modern theology" primarily because he shifted the basis of the Christian faith from the Bible to "religious experience."[361] This cultural shift is significant because it made the Bible's teachings irrelevant if one helped one's fellow man. It was the crux of liberalism. Personal belief (with the basic denial of the Bible's truths) as long as one is sincere and active in helping others. Shelley surprisingly indicates how social ministry was not born with the 20th-century movement:

"The Social Gospel, emphasized by evan-gelists of the 19th century in some manner, did not ignore ministering to people in their needs. These emphases, biblically based as an outgrowth of Scripture, were prevalent in their ministries. The

---

[359] Ibid
[360] Ibid
[361] Ibid, 423

prophets of the Social Gospel drew upon a range of these sources. Revivalism itself, which under Dwight L. Moody became heavily individualistic, had originally had a vision for a moral and Christian America. Before the Civil War, revivals and reforms went hand in hand. Charles Finney, for example, encouraged his converts to move from the personal regeneration experience to the social mission of the antislavery crusade. Social Gospel leaders also read the works of the European Christian Socialists: J.F. D. Maurice, Charles Kingsley, and others."[362]

It seemed now, with the rise of liberalism, that the conservatives were unconcerned about social action, and the liberals were the only ones who were. This generalization was a fatal mistake since the conservatives were concerned about mankind's greatest need: The salvation of his soul.

## D. Ecumenism

Ecumenism is a movement that tries to unite all denominations and groups. Its fault lies in a watering down of biblical principles and not using biblical authority and the New Birth as a basis for this union. The World Council of Churches has been at the heart of this movement. They teach a Universal Church concept and look to one Church.

Thus, as the 1970s closed, the ecumenical spirit in the World Council of Churches apparently had turned to social concerns – at times employing overt political instruments– as the primary

---

[362] Shelley, 434

expression of Christian unity. Among conservative evangelicals, the aim was the restoration of evangelism to its central place in the Church's mission, with the hope that unity would follow.[363] The controversy continued as its advocates had formulated it. It was the concern for social action contrasted with the need for salvation of those who were not Christians. The struggle still goes on today.

Common ground with these movements has led to giving ground regarding the basic teachings of the Christian faith. The Bible does not have authority, and man determining his fate is an empty emphasis in the social gospel. When someone comes to Christ in one of these movements, it illustrates how we cannot live right without a personal relationship with God.

Still, Christians need to understand what has shaped our culture today and how these influences have played an important part in our dismissing God from being a major part of our culture and, in essence, our lives. Yet, we are not hopeless. All the good History of Christianity is helpful; it allows us to answer these questions and offers the understanding that God is eternal and not bound by discoveries and doubts about Him. Instead, He is eternal, infinite, immortal, and all modern man's attempts will be answered one day concerning the truth of God's Word and its teaching.

---

[363] Ibid, 470

# Chapter 24

# Evangelical Christian Movements That Have Shaped Us

Modern man was not left to himself in the 20th century. What has evolved to the present day proves that we need God and His presence in our present world more than ever. The Christian message would not die but live through those who supported it. Instead of denying the faith because of the new challenges and questions, Bible-believing Christians tackled these happenings. Other leaders and movements from the Christian world aptly brought truth to modern man's questions about God, faith, and His Word.

The Christian world rose to the challenges it faced and offered these alternatives and emphasis to the criticisms facing its message in the modern world. Some of these alternatives, as well as places of struggle, are presented in this chapter.

# A. Fundamentalism

Fundamentalism is a reaction to Liberalism. R.A. Torrey supervised the writing of *The Fundamentals*, which was the basic literary work of the movement.[364] The introduction of this work indicated conservatives were not standing still as they watched the world change around them. They could scholarly answer critics because of the hope within them (I Pet.3:15). It was a resounding answer to liberalism's skepticism and questions from the firm foundation of the Bible and its answers to their accusations.

Fundamentalism featured a return to biblical fundamentals and literal interpretation of Scripture, the deity of Christ, His virgin birth, the atoning sacrifice of Christ, His bodily resurrection, and the physical return of Christ to earth. This movement helped save many mainline denominations from the plague of liberalism. It is especially prevalent in conservative Christian groups such as Independent Baptists and many Southern Baptists.[365]

The challenge for contemporary Christians with traditional, orthodox loyalties is to remain faithful in three things: (1) the confession that revelation is essentially outside of us in the Bible and in Jesus Christ, the incarnate Son of the Trinity; (2) faithful reflection on God in his being as

---

[364] R.A. Torrey editor, *The Fundamentals*.: (Testimony Publishing Company: Chicago. 1910), 4.
[365] What the Conservatives espoused and the groups affected most by the influence of fundamentalism.

he is in his holy immensity; and (3) living in a manner, by the Holy Spirit, that is consistent with Jesus' ethical teaching. Karl Barth's writings are listed and explained by Bingham:

"Theologians for conservative theology now rose and defended it skillfully. Karl Barth (1886-1968), a Swiss Reformed pastor and theologian, emphasized the first of these three main points. Against liberal Protestantism, he stressed that because of humanity's depravity, humans are fully dependent upon the revelation of the supreme, transcendent God in Jesus Christ, the Word of God. A religion based in subjective experience is impossible. God is not a universal human consciousness. Barth began his polemic with his *Commentary on Romans* (1919) and systematized his theology in the thirteen volumes of his *Church Dogmatics* (1932-1967)."[366]

Barth is not a solid spokesman for Conservatives. Still, his scholarly work proved that understanding and accentuating the truths of Scripture is not reserved for liberal critics of the Bible. Bingham reveals the reaction of fundamentalism to liberalism:

As a result of the perceived advance of modernity, evangelicals (fundamentalists) entered into combat with modernists. The modernists attempted to reinterpret classical orthodoxy in a manner inoffensive to modern minds, often rejecting elements of that orthodoxy completely. The fundamentalists tried to reclaim American

---

[366]Bingham, 152

society. Two things happened. First, some fundamentalists gave up and gave in, and several mainline denominations became modern. Second, staunch fundamentalists separated from mainline denominations and formed independent churches and parachurch ministries, thereby forming a fundamentalist subculture outside the larger modernist culture. Fundamentalists surrendered the universities to the modernists and formed their own institutions of education.[367]

The institutions formed stated an opposition to liberalism and its denial of Scripture.

# B. Theological Education

The battleground for the message of the Bible is centered in seminaries and Bible colleges. The 20th century witnessed a shift in the majority of the schools to a moderate or a liberal stance. Other schools like Biola and Southwestern Baptist Theological Seminary stood against such attacks on Biblical authority and the Orthodox faith.

The Southern Baptist Convention was the mainline denomination that had a turnaround in its seminaries so that Biblical Inerrancy was the standard, and schools taught what was more in line with what the members of the churches who were supporting the schools believed.

Several colleges were separated from the convention, and splinter groups were formed. However, the conservatives won the Battle for the Bible. The denomination became more

---

[367] Ibid, 163

conservative through its leaders and schools[368] A conservative resurgence was proved by the Southern Baptist Convention leaders, who were elected primarily as presidents in other positions. The growth of churches throughout the denomination and fundamental churches stood for biblical authority. The movement served as a rebuttal of the liberal view that the Bible was outdated and unsuitable for modern man. Much of their growth came from evangelism and confidence in the gospel they believed and preached. This resolve saved the denomination from liberalism.

## C. Liberalism and Its Effect on Denominations

The effect of liberalism took its toll, however, on mainline denominations that wavered in their allegiance to the Bible and truth. The shift became massive in the 60s, with the clash of values in America and the changing cultural climate.

A strange phenomenon took place in liberal denominations. People in churches disagreed with their denominations, schools, and clergy from those schools, yet they stayed in their churches. The denominations began to decline because of skepticism about the Bible, and they got more out of touch with biblical morality as they began to accept homosexuality as normal, performing weddings for homosexual couples and even admitting homosexual clergy. Abortion was viewed

---

[368] Perception of the author attending three Southern Baptist seminaries, graduating from two, and serving as a trustee for ten years at Southwestern Baptist Theological Seminary

as a right, and many people in these churches were unconverted.[369] The opposite of church growth indicated a contrast between liberalism and conservativism in the churches. The loss of membership and doubt engendered by the left-leaning churches did not bode well for their denominations built on the basic denial of conservative views of Scripture.

# D. Evangelicalism

Evangelicalism arose out of the eighteenth-century revivals taking place in Britain and their colonies. It is a movement essentially connected to Puritanism and Pietism. American evangelicalism, with its distinctive history, looks back to its British footing and continues to experience important influences from the evangelicalism of England. Throughout the world today, there are 211 million evangelicals. Bingham describes five key convictions of the Evangelical movement:

"Five convictions are at the base of the faith of those aligned with the Evangelical Movement. First, they believe the Bible is the supreme authority for faith and practice. Second, they believe in the essential of new birth, an experience of conversion through grace. Third, they believe in the centrality of the redeeming work of Christ. Fourth, they believe in the pressing need to evangelize the world. Fifth, they believe the Church is a community of believers indwelt by the Holy Spirit. These convictions, to one degree or another,

---

[369] The evidence is seen in declining membership, attendance and empty Churches

have their roots in the classical Protestant doctrines of the Reformation (salvation-church-Bible). Thus, the seedbed of what was to come was from the Protestant Reformation."[370]

Many congregations and denominations welcomed these truths because they strongly stood against liberal theology and its effect. Bingham highlights notable theologians in the Conservative movement in the 20th Century:

"Conservatives like Carl F. H. Henry (1913-2003) challenged Christians toward academic excellence and sensitivity toward the needs of a hurting society. They challenged Christians to engage with the modern culture from a conservative viewpoint and minister mercifully to its needs without being silent about or modifying conversion or classical orthodoxy. From within Britain, too, evangelicals such as the New Testament scholar F. F. Bruce (1910-1991), the pastor John R. W. Stott (1921 - 2011), and the theologian J. I. Packer (1926-2020) contributed to the betterment of evangelicalism."[371]

Conservative theologians did not run and hide. They stood up to perceived attacks on their faith with scholarly and logical answers.

Shelley believes Pietism is one of the forerunners of Evangelical Christianity in that it crossed denominational barriers. It emphasizes a personal relationship with Christ, which is at the

---

[370] Bingham, 161-162
[371] Ibid, 164

forefront of modern evangelicalism. He says, "In this sense, Pietism was the fountain of all modern revivals. It set the experience of new life in Christ as the center of the Christian message and ministry. For this reason, it is impossible to think of evangelical Christianity today without the imprint of Pietism."[372] The main teaching of Pietism is that Christianity is a personal religion centered on the abiding presence of the Holy Spirit in the believer's life. He inspires great exploits and leads believers to attempt great exploits and be controlled by the Spirit as we serve and minister in Christ's name.

Pietism assumed the existence of the Institutional Church. It made no frontal attacks upon it. But it shifted what was essential to Christianity – the new birth and the spiritual life - from the traditional state churches to intimate fellowship groups of voluntary associations of believers.

Pietism lives on not only in the Moravian denomination but also in evangelical Christianity at large, the spiritual descendants of John Wesley and George Whitefield.[373] Instead of weakening local churches, Pietism strengthened them. It brought to the realization that one's personal religion is expressed best with others in Christ's body and to a needy world in which one ministers.

---

[372] Shelley, 348
[373] Ibid, 349

# E. The Religious Right and Moral Revival

The latter part of the 20th century featured a move to politically organize and be influential in issues relating to personal morality and values. The secular society and left-leaning leaders clashed with traditional morality and forced moral reform to be the watchword for who believers supported.

First evident in the Moral Majority, the movement spread to other areas. Many believe it was the primary reason Ronald Regan was elected over Jimmy Carter, who had professed faith in Christ but governed against some Christian values. The Evangelical Christian vote, as it was also called, has evolved and most recently was prevalent in the elections in the 21$^{st}$ century and under the banner of being part of the vast Red State voter coalition.

Issues like Abortion, Homo-sexual marriage, and suppression of religious liberty are the main issues that galvanized this group and continue to hold them together to this day.[374] Such a movement was needed to counter the criticism that Conservative Churches and denominations were not active in social issues and what was perceived by conservatives as standing up for moral values, which modern society has challenged and sought to change.

---

[374] These ethical challenges give an understanding of the issues and activities of the Religious Right and Conservative Movement

# F. The Charismatic Movement

Bingham gives the origin and progress of the modern Charismatic Movement:

"With a revival in 1906, we can associate the dynamic inauguration of Pentecostalism. William J. Seymour (1870-1922), an African American minister of the gospel mission on Azusa Street in Los Angeles, California, began the fundamental Charismatic revivals. The movement, emphasizing the Spirit, sign gifts, supernaturalism, evangelism, worship, Bible study, and social sympathies, although starting slowly, developed into one of the largest movements of twentieth-century Christianity. The emphases of the movement brought forth Pentecostal denominations (for example, Assemblies of God) and found adherents within all mainline Protestant denominations and Roman Catholicism (Charismatic Christians)."[375]

The Charismatic movement can cross denominational barriers because of its emphasis on experience over biblical viewpoints that are open to interpretation and witnessed by the many types of denominations and Churches.

The movement has evolved from Pentecostal people who were quite separate and noticeable in their way of worship to mainline Churches. Christian TV was a boon to this group, but it was also a problem when some high-profile leaders, such as Jim Baker and Jimmy Swaggert, had moral problems.

---

[375] Bingham, 147

The Charismatic movement emphasizes unknown tongues, healing, demon exorcism, and the prosperity gospel in the last few decades. The group is heavy on personal experience but not given to much Biblical exposition. They can hinder evangelism by demonstrating a certain type of Christianity and claiming that non-Charismatics are not involved with and are not excited to witness for the Lord in this manner. These common marks and individuals are prominent in the recent Charismatic Movement of the last half of the 20th Century and into the recent one. Unfortunately, this so-called evidence of the Spirit's work has also brought division in churches, unwilling to accept the practices in churches that do not believe in them or do not allow such practices publicly in worship.

H. Great Crusade Efforts

Billy Sunday (1862-1935) was a famous baseball player who was saved from alcoholism when he accepted Christ in front of a rescue mission, listening to a Salvation Army band. He devoted his life to preaching the gospel and fighting alcohol. Cities would build tabernacles, and people would come forward to hit the "sawdust trail in his crusades.[376] Billy Sunday's conversion and impact made a definite difference in combating the liquor industry and reaching people for Christ in cities.

Sunday fought alcohol and was a strong force for prohibition. He was famous for his theatrics

---

[376] William Ellis, *Billy Sunday: The Man and His Message*, I.T. Myers: N.P., 1936, 50-52, 158-166.

while preaching and his dramatic delivery. He invited people to get on the wagon against alcohol. Many communities reported fewer accidents and deaths after a Sunday crusade came through.[377] This freedom from drunkenness has proven to make workers and their companies more prosperous and productive, as Sunday indicated in his sermons by figures he gave.

Dr. Wilbur Chapman tutored Sunday, and the younger preacher took over much of his ministry after he could not continue. Sunday was also a great proponent of war bonds and support of troops in World War I.[378] With little theological training in seminary or Bible College, he had a productive ministry, influencing people for good, and was a popular preacher for decades.

He was threatened in some of his crusades but preached valiantly. Noted for his wit and rapid-fire delivery, he was the first 20th-century preacher to take crusade evangelism to a different level. He blazed the trail for another evangelist from North Carolina.[379] The stage seemed set for another evangelist who would succeed Sunday by even greater proportions.

Billy Graham (1920-2019) was one of the most famous evangelists of the 20th century. As a teenager in North Carolina, he experienced salvation by listening to evangelist Mordecai

---

[377] Ibid, 91-97
[378] Ibid, 54, 508-509
[379] Ibid, 508

Ham.[380] His conversion was unnoticeable at the time. What became of his life was truly an amazing story.

Graham's ministry took off in Los Angeles and expanded to some of the largest crusades worldwide that the world has ever seen. He has taken advantage of the theological advances of the 20th century to have a worldwide impact for Christ.[381] Graham did not realize the effect his ministry would have during that first successful crusade. It was a kickoff to decades of crusades that spilled over to every continent. Bingham applauds Graham with a tribute to him through what God accomplished in his ministry:

"As a minister and evangelist, Graham excelled in his vision to reach the world for Christ to such vast proportions. Though he began his evangelistic ministry in 1944, a campaign in Los Angeles in 1949 thrust him into the national spotlight. He founded his own evangelistic association and radio ministry in 1950 and furthered his ministry by writing. He is known not only for his giftedness in evangelism but also for his service to the executive branch of the United States government, his participation in international evangelistic conferences, his willingness to work with a diversity of traditions, and his enduring integrity."[382]

---

[380] Billy Graham, *Just as I AM*, (Harper-Collins: San Francisco, 1997) 29-31.
[381] Ibid, 143-158
[382] Bingham, 164

The many facets of Graham's ministry continued to grow and produce unbelievable results worldwide.

Graham has been a confidant to presidents and has been sought after all over the world in crusade evangelism. He has authored many books and worked steadily with his Minster of Music Cliff Barrows and soloist George Beverly Shea for over six decades. Only eternity will reveal the multitudes who have come to Christ through the ministry of Billy Graham.[383] His ministry was a dominant force in the 20th century, proving that the gospel preached in any century could still change lives through conversion to Christ and His salvation.

Evangelical Christians feature many streams that have contributed to present-day Christianity. The challenge is still more evident in preaching the gospel to the whole world so that all can come to Christ.

New movements and leaders have continued the call of Christ to preach the gospel to the whole world. Instead of disintegrating, the Christian faith has become a bedrock for those looking for more than this world offers. For this reason, those standing for the truth of the Bible have been active and in the middle of all the questioning and warfare of our present day. God has not abandoned us but is making Himself more evident as humanity's needs and helplessness grow. The answer is clear and certain in the Bible and with 20 centuries of

---

[383] Ibid 164-165

Christian History to back it up as a transforming presence in our age.

# Chapter 25

# Important Emphasis in 20th-Century Christianity by the Decades and into the 21st

The 20th Century helps us to see how we have evolved in history concerning the major issues we have confronted and will continue to confront. Because so much has happened in the last century and this one, it is good to see challenges, new theories, beliefs, and answers to these challenges continuously.

With all that has happened in the modern age, it is easy to get overwhelmed and the events incomprehensible. Clarification is needed by breaking down some major events and movements pertaining to Christian History over the decades. The listing is not an attempt to gain a total understanding of every event and movement but to call attention to them. Understanding how these movements and events have changed society and what is necessary to know about them is important and helpful.

# 00-10 Social Gospel and Fundamentalist Conflict

The Liberal/Fundamentalist conflict burst upon churches at the beginning of the century. The social gospel stands in opposition to the evangelism of fundamentalists.

Professor Martin Marty suggests that we call the parties "Public Protestants" and "Private" Protestants." His terms arise from the fact that one group spoke of Social Christianity, Social Gospel, Social Service, and so on, while the other, often using the term "evangelical," stressed the need for individual salvation.[384] The difference in churches and denominations is stark concerning these differences in theology and emphasis. This difference has caused many conservative churches to ask if these congregations and denominations dominated by liberalism are churches at all.

# 10's- The Great War, Disruption, Birth of Communism, Changing of Millennial Views

The Marxist-Leninist theory claimed that religion is a false consciousness, an illusory reflection of the world resulting from class divisions. When society is restored to a "normal" state in communism, they believe religion will die a natural death. That is the theory. And yet,

---

[384] Shelley, 413

communists actively struggle against religion. The party regards itself as the embodiment of the ideals of Marxism and cannot allow any part of society to operate outside its control.[385] The normal state of the world was dominated in the 20th century by violence, war, and destruction. This continual warfare is not the normal state of the world and is far from what God intended it to be without a Christian witness leading to change for the good.

The Great War caused many to change millennial views, previously feeling that the Second Coming of Christ would come through gospel preaching. The post-millennial view is especially a victim of teaching that the world will improve before Jesus returns. Regardless of one's millennial viewpoint, the Bible does not change but has an eternal and life-changing message.

## 20's- Alternative Values, Prohibition, Scopes Trial Victory for Evolutionism

New values were explored after America's venture abroad. The roaring twenties and the opposition to prohibition were notable for wild living and crime.

William Jennings Bryan wrote that those who labored for Prohibition "are helping to create conditions which will bring the highest good to the greatest number, for it is not injustice to any man to refuse him permission to enrich himself by injuring his fellowmen."[386] Prohibition was a hot-

---

[385] Ibid, 445
[386] Ibid, 456

button issue that countered the Scopes Trial influence, which opened the door to evolution and eventually being taught in schools. Although Prohibition did not last and was repealed, it had a noble goal to save families from poverty and harm. It would eventually help the scourge of crime in cities, although speak-easies were born still pedaling illegal alcohol.

## 30's- Secularism, Industrialism, Spreads, Neo-Orthodoxy as an Accommodation

After the Scopes trial, accommodations were birthed, which led to theistic evolution and modification of orthodoxy, called Neo-Orthodoxy. These actions represented a surrender to liberalism.

The 30s represented rapid industrialism and featured many leaving behind traditional values developed in the rural areas.

Shelley told of "industrialism's changes when he revealed, "A second shock to traditional faith came from the increasing industrialization of American society and the rush to the cities. Small towns became big cities overnight. People came from America's hinterland, Germany, Norway, Italy, and other European countries. Most new immigrants brought religious opinions alien to the traditional way Protestant Americans viewed their country and the Bible."

America eventually topped the 19th-century immigration totals. The chaotic state of the world and the opportunities presented here led to mass migration. As immigrants brought their religious heritage with them, America was becoming more religiously diverse, and the old world's view of religion was clashing with this country's perspective on churches and their place in society.[387]

The German Churches began to grapple with the threats of dictatorship under Hitler. In May 1934, the Confessing Church spelled out its theological convictions in *The Barmen Declaration.* Largely written by Karl Barth, the Declaration called the German Churches back to the central truths of Christianity and rejected totalitarian claims of the state.[388] It was a tough time to cry for religious freedom against the most brutal dictatorship in the 20th century that took over churches not loyal to it. It resulted in theologians like Dietrich Bonhoeffer's execution against such tyranny.

## 40's- Patriotism and Sacrifice Exhibited in WWII and Thereafter

Great heroism was exhibited by those who fought in World War II. Some have called those who gave great self-sacrifice in our military "the greatest generation." Many changed the world, and the world was changed forever. Many who survived were forged in the furnace of affliction to be productive members of society. Devotion to God and reliance on him was at the center of turmoil in

---

[387] Ibid, 412
[388] Ibid, 443

this decade. President Franklin Roosevelt prayed on national TV as our troops attacked Normandy on D-Day 1944.[389]

# 50's- Age of Innocence, Traditionalism, Rock Music Begins its Influence

The country was at peace, and the traditional family and values reigned supreme. However, rock music and new forms of entertainment, such as television, challenged traditional ways of thinking and living.

# 60's- Clash of Values, Civil Rights Movement, Liberalism Affects Major Denominations

The '60s were a decade of turmoil. New immoral values were gaining acceptance. Civil rights were still not fully granted, and a struggle ensued. Bingham shares about Martin Luther King's leadership in Civil Rights:

"In the twentieth century, things had improved little, if at all. In an environment of pervasive social injustice Martin Luther King Jr. (1929-1968) became the visible, leading voice against racial discrimination through nonviolence. Assassinated in Memphis, Tennessee, on April 4, 1968, at the age of thirty-nine, King had rallied the

---

[389] The National WII Museum This text was originally published by the Franklin Delano Roosevelt Presidential Library & Museum New Orleans, LA
https://www.nationalww2museum.org/war/articles/franklin-d-roosevelts-d-day-prayer-june-6-1944< ND., NA.

conscience of the nation against the practice of segregation, the tolerance of poverty, and the furtherance of war. His popularity illustrated the need to ensure equal rights for all races. King, the son of a Baptist minister, had been touched by the evangelical spirituality of the African American tradition."[390]

King's death highlighted the tensions that boiled over in the later part of the decade after seeing a president and his brother assassinated. Uncertainty reigned supreme as a new decade approached.

Several mainline denominations had been facing encroaching liberalism but made a radical departure from the faith of their fathers during this time.

## 70's- Super Churches, Bus Ministry, Feminist Movement, Roe v. Wade Decision

Evangelical Churches began to grow rapidly on the heels of the Jesus movement. Bus Ministries were huge and expanded. Jimmy Carter claimed to be a born-again Christian and won many evangelical votes just stating this.

The Supreme Court legalized abortion in January 1973. The Feminist movement grew, and several mainline denominations ordained women as ministers and pastors of congregations. The freedom of abortion made it available everywhere. Great disagreements arose over its legalization. The law

---

[390] Bingham, 160

allowing abortion as a nationwide freedom returned to the states, with the original decision by the Supreme Court overturned 50 years later.

## 80's- Religious Right, Corporate Profits, Boom and Downfall, Cold War Ends

Christians could not appeal to the State to control morality and force people to go to Church. They did organize, however, into voting coalitions that supported only candidates representing their moral viewpoint. The Moral Majority and other conservative groups were formed with pastors and churches in the middle of them.

However, the primary means of still winning people to Christ was through evangelistic efforts, not governmental edicts. Shelley relates the most proven method of moral change through evangelism when he says, "Christians could no longer appeal to the arm of power to suppress such heresies. So, many of them turned instead to the apostles' way of prayer and preaching. The result was a series of evangelical revivals, chiefly similar to Pietism, Methodism, and the Great Awakening. Evangelicals tried to restore God to public life by preaching and personal conversions."[391]

Maintaining a Christian witness with all the changes in modern society was an uphill climb. There were many distractions to compete with and no public pressure to get involved in Church.

---

[391] Shelley, 494

Communist countries were now open to evangelization because of the fall of Communism in Europe. Many Christian organizations took advantage of this situation, and there was more openness in Eastern Europe than in America, which had churches and, hopefully, a religious influence.

# 90's- Seeker Sensitive Churches, Contemporary Worship, Non-Denominationalism

As the culture became more secular, innovative ways were used to seek and reach them. Non-denominationalism was in because some churches didn't want to be as overt as they were.

The seeker, as so-called, was the object of church worship, featuring radical departures in the style of worship and expressions of praise.[392] These seeker-sensitive churches changed much of how the church had been doing church.

# 00-10- Red State Voters, War on Christianity

Christianity versus Secularism, ACLU, Gay Marriage Struggle

The new millennium brought hope and promise as well as fear. 911, with the massacre of over 3,000 and the destruction of the Twin Towers in New York, revealed the insecurity all felt. Uncertainty

---

[392] Got Questions? Should a Church be seeker sensitive? https://www.gotquestions.org/seeker-sensitive-Church.html, NA, ND

in the world makes the certain message of the gospel more relevant than it has ever been

The election of George W. Bush was attributed basically to Red State voters who voted for moral values and against Gay Marriage.[393]

Many shots are being fired at Christians, trying to take away religious freedom, but the truth of God cannot be bound till Christ returns. Our faith is centered in Christ, and He will reign supreme one day as the final fulfillment of our faith. The History of Christianity is all about Him and His work, never to be ignored.

## 10-24- Gay Marriage is legalized, with a decline in Church attendance among Youth and College Students.

Rowe vs Wade is overturned, and there is a sharp disagreement between secular and spiritual.

The COVID-19 virus was worldwide, forcing shutdowns in many public places and businesses and hurting owners. The pandemic made the populace more reliant on the government and called into question the right to assemble as churches over government decrees.

Churches have become loose and not as old-fashioned. Sex change operations have become

---

[393] Louis Jacobson, U.S. News and World https://www.usnews.com/news/best-states/articles/2024-05-07/divided-nation-are-americas-best-states-red-or-blue, Report May 7, 2024 , (Accessed October 31, 3024).

more popular. Children are encouraged to question their gender identity.

God is still on his throne, though, and Bible-believing Churches are still preaching the gospel despite the threat of wars. These fears come particularly in the Middle East regarding Israel's attack and her enemies, Russia's war with Ukraine, and China's big build-up.

Donald Trump was elected president in 2024, returning to Washington for the second time, interrupted by the election he lost in 2020. Many look at this election as a return in some way to more conservative views on moral issues

The gospel will still be preached by those churches faithful to God until Jesus shall return. They stand in the gap between immorality, false beliefs, and the truth of God's Word.

We close our study of Christian History, understanding that not all events that may have shaped it were covered. Yet, this work has tried to break it down and see what I deem valuable to your knowledge of how God has worked in every age through Christ to the present day.

In the end, it has been and always will be HIS STORY. It is all about Jesus. If our study has drawn us closer to Jesus and His story, then much has been accomplished. Our purpose for living as Christians in the world is to glorify Him and let others know about Him. The Christian events through the ages are not just for information not previously known, but to know Him personally, for whom to know is eternal life.

Let us close with Bruce Shelley's description and value of studying Christ's story:

No person in recorded history has influenced more people in as many conditions over so long as Jesus Christ. The shades of his image seem to shift with the needs of men: The Jewish Messiah of the believing remnant, the Wisdom of the Greek apologist, the Cosmic King of the Imperial Church, the Heavenly Logos of the orthodox councils, the World Ruler of the papal courts, the monastic Model of apostolic poverty, and the personal Savior of evangelical revivalists.

Truly, He is a man for all time. In a day when many regard him as irrelevant, a relic of a quickly discarded past. Church History provides a quiet testimony that Jesus Christ will not disappear from the scene. His title may change, but his truth endures for all generations.[394]

The History of Christianity has featured a variety of beliefs and practices in every century since Jesus' ministry and sacrifice for sin on the cross. His resurrection resulted in the Church's commissioning to go into the world with His gospel. The message has been successful and God-ordained in a wonderful way. Such a pattern confirms how New Testament Churches are a divine organization God has preserved through the ages.

We learn from this study how these beliefs and practices have brought us to where we are today. Despite all the corruption and error, God has

---

[394] Shelley, 495

a pattern of truth that many have followed and preserved for us a faith that was "once delivered to the saints." (Jude 3) One cannot help but exclaim with Paul as they see how God has preserved this body of truth and changed the world through the gospel of Christ: "Unto Him be glory in the Church by Christ Jesus throughout all ages, world without end. Amen." (Eph. 3:21)

# Bibliography

## Articles, Addresses


Barnes, Frank, "Ten False Teachings of Mormonism," *Church Membership Orientation for Baptist Churches.* Longview, Texas: The Shop at Arpop, 1975.

Briggs, John, Tim Dowley ed., "Early English Baptists, *"The History of Christianity*. Oxford, England: Lion Publishers 1977.

Brown, Colin, Tim Dowley ed., "Fredrich Schleiermacher," *The History of Christianity*. Oxford, England: Lion Publishers, 1977.

Donnely, John, Tim Dowley ed. "The Jesuits," *The History of Christianity*. Oxford, England: Lion Publishers, 1977.

Lawson, Steve, Biographical Presentation of John Calvin, by at The Shepherd's Conference. Grace Community Church April 2012.

Smith, A., Tim Dowley ed., "Christian Ascetics and Monks," *The History of Christianity*. Lion Publishers: Oxford, England: 1977.

Wood, Skevington, Tim Dowley ed., "John and Charles Wesley," *The History of Christianity*. Lion Publishers: Oxford, England, 1977.


## Bible Version


The Bible, King James Version. Nashville, TN: Holman Bible, 1999.

# Books

A Kempis, Thomas. (Translated by Richard Whitford). *The Imitation of Christ*. New York: Pocket Books, 1954.

Abanes Richard. *Becoming Gods: A Closer Look at 21st-Century Mormonism*. Eugene, OR: Harvest House, 2004.

Armstrong, O.K. and Marjorie, *The Baptists in America*. Garden New York City: Doubleday, 1975.

Bainton, Roland. *Christendom: A Short History of Christianity and Its Impact on Western Civilization*, Volume 1. New York: Harper, 1964.

______________. *A Short History of Christianity and Its Impact on Western Civilization*, Volume 2. New York: Harper, 1966.

______________. *Here I Stand, A life of Martin Luther*. Nashville: Abingdon Press: 1950.

Beale, David. *Baptist History in England and America*: *Personalities, Positions, and Practices*. Maitland, FL: Xulon Press: 2018.

Bingham, Jeffery. *Pocket History of the Christian Church*. Downers Grove, IL., 2002.

Cowdrey, Wayne. Davis Howard A. & Scales, Donald R. *Who Really Wrote the Book of Mormon?* Santa Ana, CA: Vision House, 1977.

Dallimore Arnold A. George Whitefield: God's Anointed Servant in the Great Revival of the

Eighteenth-Century Volume 2. Wheaton, Ill: Crossway, 1990.

Edwards, Jonathan, revised and corrected by Edmund Hickman *The Works of Jonathan Edwards*. Carlisle, PA: The Banner of Truth Trust, reprinted 1984.

Ellis, William. *Billy Sunday: The Man and His Message*. U.S.A: I.T. Myers, 1936.

Estep, William. *The Anabaptist Story*. Grand Rapids: Eerdmans, 1975.

Fish, Bruce, and Becky. *George Whitefield, Pioneering Evangelist.* Uhrichsville, OH: Barbour Books, 2000.

Fox, John. Fox's *Book of Martyrs, or The Acts and Monuments of the Christian Church*. Philadelphia: J.B. Smith, 1856.

Gonzalez, Justo L. *The Story of Christianity* Volume 1. San Francisco: Harper and Rowe, 1984.

Graham, Billy. *Just As I AM*. San Francisco: Harper-Collins,1997.

Hoffer, Peter. James *When Benjamin Franklin Met The Reverend Whitefield*: *Enlightenment, Revival and the Power of the Printed Word*. Baltimore: John Hopkins University Press, 2011.

Kidd, Thomas S. *George Whitefield: America's Spiritual Founding Father*. New Haven, CT: Yale University Press, 2014.

Latourette, Kenneth Scott. *A History of Christianity: A Revised edition, Volume I: Beginnings to 1500*. New York: Harper Row, 1975.

__________________________. *A History of Christianity*: A Revised edition, Volume II: *1500 to 1975*. New York: Harper Row,1975.

Leith, John ed. *Creeds of the Church*: A Reader in Christian Doctrine from the Bible to the Present, The Revised Edition. Atlanta: John Knox Press, 1963.

Lewis, Peter. *The Genius of Puritanism*. Morgan, PA: Soli Deo Gloria Publications, 1997.

Marsden, George. *Jonathan Edwards, A Life.* New Haven, CT: Yale University Press, 2003.

Martin, Walter. *The Kingdom of the Cults,* "Jehovah's Witnesses and the Watchtower Bible and Tract Society." Minneapolis: Bethany House, 2003.

__________________. *The Maze of Mormonism*. Santa Ana, California: Vison House, 1962.

McBeth, Leon. *The Baptist Heritage*. Nashville: Broadman, 1987.

Meade, Frank. *The Ten Decisive Battles of Christianity*. New York: Bobbs-Merrill, Co, 1936.

McNeill, John T. *The History and Character of Calvinism*. Oxford, England: Oxford University Press, 1954.

Murray Iain, H. *Jonathan Edwards, A New Biography*. Carlisle, PA:  Banner of Truth Trust, 1987.

Nelson, Dan. *A Burning and Shining Light: The Testimony and Witness of George Whitefield*. Lifesong Publishers, 2017.

__________. *Baptist Biographies and Happenings in American History*. Fort Myers, FL: Faithful Life Publishers, 2018.

__________. *Early Baptists: A Comparative Study of the Anabaptists and English Baptist Movements*. Fort Myers, FL: Faithful Life Publishers, 2021.

Neuman, Albert. *A Manual of Church History* Volume 1. *Ancient and Medieval Church History*. Valley Forge, PA: Judson Press, 1979.

Reed, David A. *Jehovah's Witnesses Answered Verse by Verse.* Grand Rapids, MI: Baker Book House, 1986.

Schaff, Philip. *History of the Christian Church* Vol. VIII. Grand Rapids, MI: Eerdmans, 1960.

Shelley, Bruce L. *Church History in Plain Language*. Dallas: Word Publishing, 1982.

Smith, John. Witnessing Effectively to Mormons. Marlowe, OK: Utah Missions, 1975.

Street, Alan. *Cult Invasion*. Dallas: Street Meetings, 1989.

Torrey, R.A. ed. *The Fundamentals*. Chicago: Testimony Publishing Company, 1904.

Vedder, Henry C. *A Short History of the Baptists*. Philadelphia: The American Baptist Publication Society, 1907.

Weaver, Daniel, J. *Becoming Anabaptist: The Origin and Significance of Sixteenth-Century Anabaptism*. 2nd ed. Scottdale, PA: Herald Press, 1987.

# Internet Sites

Adam Augustyn. *Encyclopedia Britannica*, John Milton, https://www.britannica.com/topic/Paradise-Lost-epic-poem-by-Milton. ND, (Accessed November 12, 2024).

Anderson-Rajkumar Evangeline, Christian History Institute, https://christianhistoryinstitute.org/magazine/article/ministry-in-killing-fields, 1992, (Accessed January 16, 2025

Bradley, Nassif. "John Chrysostom: The Golden-Mouth Preacher," https://www.equip.org/articles/john-chrysostom-the-golden-mouth-preacher/. August 27, 2021, (Accessed, October 11, 2024).

Brandon, Steve "Enjoying His Grace and Extending His Glory," https://enjoyinghisgrace.wordpress.com/2016/01/27/the-plow-boy/, January 27, 2016, (Accessed November 12, 2024).

Britannica Procon. Org. "Religion in the Original 13 Colonies," https://undergod.procon.org/religion-in-the-original-13-colonies/, Jan 6, 2009, NA, (Accessed Oct. 27, 2024

Brom, Robert, Catholic Tract Society, "Strategies of the Jehovah's Witnesses," https://www.catholic.com/tract/strategies-of-the-jehovahs-witnesses," August 10, 2004, (Accessed October 29, 2024).

Christian History Magazine. "George Whitefield, did you Know?"

https://christianhistoryinstitute.org/magazine/article/george-whitefield-did-you-know, N.A, Article in Christian History magazine, Issue 38, 1993. (Accessed November 19, 2024).

Christian Science: "Online Worship Service," https://www.christianscience.com/publications-and-activities/online-services-and-events/online-sunday-Church-service, ND, NA, (Accessed October 29, 2024).

Church of Jesus Christ of Latter-Day Saints, "The Manifesto and the End of Plural Marriage," (https://www.Churchofjesuschrist.org/study/manual/gospel-topics-essays/race-and-the-priesthood?lang=eng), ND, NA, (Accessed October 29, 2024).

Criswell, W.A., W.A. Criswell Sermon Library, Dallas, TX, Sam Hull administrator: "St. Patrick was a Baptist Preacher," 1958 http://www.wacriswell.com/sermons/1958/st-patrick-was-a-baptist-preacher/, (Accessed December 27, 2015).

Emory Elliott, "The Legacy of Puritanism," October 24, 2014, https://nationalhumanitiescenter.org/tserve/eighteen/ekeyinfo/legacy.htm. (Accessed October 2024).

"Emancipation of the Freed," https://emancipationofthefreed.blogspot.com/2007/01/john-leonard-dober-and-david-nitschman.html, January 21, 2007. NA., (Accessed November 21, 2024).

Farrell, Steve ed. "John Leland: Tireless Champion for Religious Liberty," *Political Sermons, Founding Era*, 1754-1841. John Leland bio https://selfeducatedamerican.com/2010/05/02/john-leland-tireless-champion-ofreligious-liberty, February 5, 2002, (Accessed April 11, 2018).

Flick, Stephen.\, "The Prayer Meeting That Saved England, Christian History Magazine." (https://christianheritagefellowship.com/prayer-meeting-that-saved-england/, December 27, 2023, (Accessed October 27, 2024).

Finney, Charles. "Who was Charles Finney"? (https://www.gotquestions.org/Charles-Finney.html), NA, ND).

Galli, Mark, "Persecution in the Early Church," Christian History Institute, https://christianhistoryinstitute.org/magazine/article/persecution-in-early-church-gallery, 1990, (Accessed, January 21, 2025).

Got Questions?" "Should a Church be seeker-sensitive?" https://www.gotquestions.org/seeker-sensitive-Church.html, NA, ND.

History of the World, "Simony" N.A., (https://www.historyworld.net/history/Papacy/543?section=1st 8thCentury https://www.britannica.com/topic/simony) NA, ND, (Accessed November 7, 2024).

History of England, "Thomas Becket." https://www.historic-uk.com/HistoryUK/HistoryofEngland/Thomas-Becket/, NA, ND, (Accessed November 9, 2024).

JSTOR Daily, "Making Sense of the Divine Right of Kings" https://daily.jstor.org/making-sense-of-the-divine-right-of-kings/, ND, (Accessed November 7, 2024).

Jacobson, Louis U., "Red or Blue States News and World Report," https://www.usnews.com/news/best-states/articles/2024-05-07/divided-nation-are-americas-best-states-red-or-blue, May 7, 2024, (Accessed October 31, 3024).

______________, "Pre-KJV English Translations," 2011https://christianhistoryinstitute.org/magazine/article/pre-kjv-english-translations, N.D., (Accessed November 11, 2024).

Lyle, David Jeffrey, "The Colosseum: Power, Brilliance, and Brutality," (https://depts.washington.edu/hrome/Authors/jimkuo2/IlColosseo/253/pub_zbpage_view.html#:~:text=Were%20Christians%20really%20fed%20to,in%20a%20less%20public%20place, Sept. 6, 2004, (Accessed October 23, 2024).

Julian, John, *"O' Sacred Head Now Wounded,"* Dictionary of Hymnology, https://hymnary.org/text/o_sacred_head_now_wounded, 1907, (Accessed, November 7.2024).

Kid's Britannica https://quotefancy.com/quote/1554685/Mary-Queen-of-Scots-I-fear-the-prayers-of-John-Knox-more-than-all-the-assembled-armies-of, NA, ND, (Accessed November 12, 2024).

Luther, Martin, The Ninety-Five Theses, The Disputation on the Power and Efficacy of Indulgences, Posted: October 31, 1517, Castle Church, Wittenberg, Germany, http://reverendluther.org/pdfs/The_Ninety-Five_Theses.pdf, (Accessed December 31, 2024).

Madsen, William, "Christo-Paganism. A Study of Mexican Religious Syncretism." New Orleans, Tulane University. Middle American Research Institute. https://ewtn.co.uk/chpop-the-amazing-life-of-saint-junipero-serra-apostle-of-california-first-saint-to-be-canonized-on-u-s-soil/, 1957, (Accessed November 14, 2024).

Martinez Rich, "The Canon of the Testament" https://www.biblicaltheology.com/Research/MartinezR01.html, 2002, (Accessed November 10, 2024).

Mass, David," The Life and Times of D.L. Moody," https://christianhistoryinstitute.org/magazine/article/life-and-times-of-moody, Christian History, Issue 25, 1990.

Mathison, Keith, Calvin and the Doctrine of Irresistible Grace, Ligonier Ministries, https://www.ligonier.org/learn/articles/john-calvin-and-doctrine-irresistible-grace, Oct 16, 2018, (Accessed November 8, 2024).

Mayflower Society, Mayflower Compact, https://themayflowersociety.org/history/the-mayflower-compact/, November 11, 1620, (Accessed December 31,2024).

Munro & Bramhall in Translations and Reprints, IV, Emperor Constantine Augustus, *Edict of Milian*, https://droitromain.univ-grenoble-alpes.fr/Anglica/ed_tolerat2_engl.htm, Philadelphia, 1898 (Accessed December 31, 2024).

Pavao, Paul. "Athenagoras," Christian History for Everyman: Christian History for Everyman. Greatest Stories Ever Told. <https://www.christian-history.org/page-name.html, 2014, (Accessed November 7, 2024).

Pruitt, Sarah, "Why the King James Bible of 1611 Remains the Most Popular Translation in History," https://www.history.com/news/king-james-bible-most-popular, Updated: July 13, 2023, | Original: March 22, 2019, (Accessed November 4, 2024).

Quora, "Why did the Watchtower Organization claim to be a prophet of God," https://www.quora.com/Why-did-the-Watchtower-Organization-claim-to-be-a-prophet-of-God-in-Apr-1-1972-p-197-WT-since-they-have-changed-many-understandings-such-as-the-generation-in-the-time-of-the-end-claiming-it-is-light-from-God), ND., NA. (Accessed October 28, 2024).

Roosevelt, Franklin Delano the National WII Museum This text was originally published by the Franklin Delano Roosevelt Presidential Library & Museum New Orleans, https://www.nationalww2museum.org/war/article

s/franklin-d-roosevelts-d-day-prayer-june-6-1944<, ND., NA.

Schleicher, Andrew, "Why the Wesley's, and others, came to be called Methodists," https://www.umc.org/en/content/why-the-wesleys-and-others-came-to-be-called-methodists#:~:text=%22These%20were%20all%20names%20foisted, and%20updated%20June%2028%2C%202023, September 21, 2015, and updated June 28, 2023, (Accessed, October 28, 2024).

The Schleitheim Confession, (Michael Sattler, alleged author. https://courses.washington.edu/hist112/SCHLEITHEIM%20CONFESSION%20OF%20FAITH.htm, 1527, Schleitheim Switzerland, (Accessed December, 31, 2024).

Sporleder, Rita, The Amazing Life of Junipero Serra, https://ewtn.co.uk/chpop-the-amazing-life-of-saint-junipero-serra-apostle-of-california-first-saint-to-be-canonized-on-u-s-soil/, June 30, (2024, Accessed October 28, 2024).

Todd Obbie Tyler, "The First Prayer in Congress," https://christianheritagefellowship.com/the-first-prayer-in-congress/, Sept 24, 2004, accessed October 27, 2024.) (https://www.obbietylertodd.com/post/a-brief-history-of-the-election-sermon-in-america. Nov 19, 2020, (Accessed October 27, 2024).

*United States Constitution, Bill of Rights, First Amendment National Archives: America's Founding Documents, Bill of Rights: A Transcription* https://www.archives.gov/contact, December 15, 1791, (Accessed December 31, 2024).

Waterworth. J., "The Jesuits," *The History of Christianity,* 420 (*Word Explain*, Contemplative Theology, Contemplating Roman Catholicism, Edited and translated by (London: Dolman,) https://www.wordexplain.com/Anathemas_and_t he_Council_of_Trent.html, 1848, ( Accessed November 8, 2024)

Wimberley, Mary "Tyndale's Will to 'One Thing' Resulted in English Bible," https://www.samford.edu/news/2009/Tyndales-Will-to-One- Thing-Resulted-in-English-Bible#:~:text=Tyndale's%20last%20words%20b efore%20being, Bible%20was%20published%20in%201611, October 30, 2009, (Accessed November 20, 2024).

Wood, Skevington, "John and Charles Wesley," *Handbook of Christianity*, Britannica Procon. Org. Religion in the Original 13 Colonies. https://undergod.procon.org/religion-in-the-original-13-colonies/, Jan 6, 2009, NA, accessed Oct. 27, 2024.

# Appendices

## Appendix A
## The Edict of Milan

Freedom of worship granted to all Christians
(AD 313)

(Munro & Bramhall in Translations and
Reprints, IV, Philadelphia, 1898, p. 29-30

The edict officially given by Constantine is an attempt at becoming a Christian by government edict. It was the first known proclamation for Christians to live peacefully and favored in a civil government. This attempt, however noble as it can be, is not how one becomes a Christian. Surely, it was acceptable to believers, although it made decisions for individuals who must come to Christ personally.

However, this decree is what many believe as truthful in sincerity. It does fall short of everyone coming to salvation in Christ. Some may very well have come to Christ through this edict. But it is the beginning of State Religion, which did more wrong than the good a decree like this may have accomplished. Religion under the control of the government is not a proven winner but a loser on many fronts.

We hear about this edict a lot. Reading the decree and seeing how this came back to work evil toward true believers who withstood the government in future history is interesting and sad. The government was in control of all the brands of religion at the time and sponsored by the existing government.

## Here is the Edict and all it entailed through its validity

When I, Constantine Augustus, as well as I, Licinius Augustus, had fortunately met near Mediolanum (Milan), and were considering everything that pertained to the public welfare and security, we thought that, among other things which we saw would be for the good of many, those regulations pertaining to the reverence of the Divinity ought certainly to be made first, so that we might grant to the Christians and to all others full authority to observe that religion which each preferred ; whence any Divinity whatsoever in the seat of the heavens may be propitious and kindly disposed to us and all who are placed under our rule.

And thus, by this wholesome counsel and most upright provision we thought to arrange that no one whatsoever should be denied the opportunity to give his heart to the observance of the Christian religion, or of that religion which he should think best for himself, so that the Supreme Deity, to whose worship we freely yield our hearts, may show in all things His usual favor and benevolence. Therefore, your Worship should know that it has pleased us to remove all conditions whatsoever, which were in the rescripts formerly given to you officially, concerning the Christians, and now any one of these who wishes to observe the Christian religion may do so freely and openly, without any disturbance or molestation.

We thought it fit to commend these things most fully to your care that you may know that we have given to those Christians free and unrestricted opportunity of religious worship. When you see that this has been granted to them by us, your Worship will know that we have also conceded to other religions the right of open and free observance of their worship for the sake of the peace of our times, that each one may have the free opportunity to worship as he pleases; this regulation is made that we may not seem to detract aught from any dignity or any religion.

Moreover, in the case of the Christians especially, we esteemed it best to order that if it happens that anyone heretofore has bought from our treasury or from anyone whatsoever, those places where they were previously accustomed to assemble, concerning which a certain decree had been made and a letter sent to you officially, the same shall be restored to the Christians without payment or any claim of recompense and without any kind of fraud or deception, Those, moreover, who have obtained the same by gift, are likewise to return them at once to the Christians. Besides, both those who have purchased and those who have secured them by gift, are to appeal to the vicar if they seek any recompense from our bounty, that they may be cared for through our clemency. All this property ought to be delivered at once to the community of the Christians through your intercession, and without delay.

And since these Christians are known to have possessed not only those places in which they were accustomed to assemble, but also other property, namely the Churches, belonging to them as a corporation and not as individuals, all these things which we have included under the above law, you will order to be restored, without any hesitation or controversy at all, to these Christians, that is to say to the corporations and their conventicles:— providing, of course, that the above arrangements be followed so that those who return the same without payment, as we have said, may hope for an indemnity from our bounty.

In all these circumstances you ought to tender your most efficacious intervention to the community of the Christians, that our command may be carried into effect as quickly as possible, whereby, moreover, through our clemency, public order may be secured. Let this be done so that, as we have said above, Divine favor towards us, which, under the most important circumstances we have already experienced, may, for all time, preserve and prosper our successes together with the good of the state. Moreover, in order that the statement of this decree of our good will may come to the notice of all, this rescript, published by your decree, shall be announced everywhere and brought to the knowledge of all, so that the decree of this, our benevolence, cannot be concealed.

https://droitromain.univ-grenoble-alpes.fr/Anglica/ed_tolerat2_engl.htm

# Appendix B

# The Ninety-five Theses by Martin Luther

## October 31, 1517, Wittenberg, Germany
## The Eve of All Saints Day, Castle Church
## Wittenberg, Germany
## For oral debate on November 1, 1517

We often hear of the nailing of the 95 theses to the Church door at Wittenberg, but many cannot recall, not many, if any, of the theses. Some of these may seem redundant, but it is helpful to see why they were instrumental in starting the Reformation.

Read them to fully understand how their posting changed not only the religious world but the world we live in.

### Luther's Invitation to Debate These Proclamations

Out of love and zeal for truth and the desire to bring it to light, the following theses will be publicly discussed at Wittenberg under the chairmanship of the reverend father, Martin Luther, Master Name of Our Lord Jesus of Arts and Sacred Theology and regularly appointed Lecturer on these subjects at that place. He requests that those who cannot be present to debate orally with us will do so by letter.

In the Christ. Amen.

The first three these statements are for discussion on the importance of God's Word in the Holy Bible for the Christian's life.

1. When our Lord and Master Jesus Christ said, "Repent" [Matthew 4:17], he willed the entire life of believers to be one of repentance.

2. This word cannot be understood as referring to the sacrament of penance, that is confession and satisfaction, as administered by the clergy.

3. Yet it does not mean solely inner repentance; such inner repentance is worthless unless it produces various outward mortifications of the flesh.

Theses #4-14 address the power of the pope, challenge the teachings of purgatory, address the corruption of the clergy, and the source of the forgiveness of sins as a direct act from God.

4. The penalty of sin remains as long as the hatred of self, that is, true inner repentance, until our entrance into the kingdom of heaven.

5. The pope neither desires nor is able to remit any penalties except those imposed by his own authority or that of the canons.

6. The pope cannot remit any guilt, except by declaring and showing that it has been remitted by God; or, to be sure, by remitting guilt in cases reserved to his judgment. If his right to grant remission in these cases were disregarded, the guilt would certainly remain unforgiven.

7. God remits guilt to no one unless at the same time he humbles him in all things and makes him submissive to his vicar, the priest.

8. The penitential canons are imposed only on the living, and, according to the canons themselves, nothing should be imposed on the dying.

9. Therefore, the Holy Spirit through the pope is kind to us insofar as the pope in his decrees always makes exception of the article of death and necessity.

10. Those priests act ignorantly and wickedly who, in the case of the dying reserve canonical penalties for purgatory.

11. Those tares of changing the canonical penalty to the penalty of purgatory were evidently sown while the bishops slept. [Matthew 13:25]

12. In former times canonical penalties were imposed, not after, but before absolutism, as tests of true contrition.

13. The dying are freed by death from all penalties, are already dead as far as the canon laws are concerned, and have a right to be released from them.

14. Imperfect piety or love on the part of a dying person necessarily brings with it great fear, and the smaller the love, the greater the fear.

Theses #15 – 82 are the core arguments by Martin Luther against indulgences and the tactics of the preachers who are selling letters of indulgence in Germany.

15. This fear of horror is sufficient in itself, to say nothing of other things, to constitute the penalty of purgatory, since it is very near the horror of despair.

16. Hell, purgatory, and heaven seem to differ the same as despair, fear, and assurance of salvation.

17. It seems as though for the souls in purgatory fear should necessarily decrease and love increase.

18. Furthermore, it does not seem proved, either by reason or Scripture, that souls in purgatory are outside the state of merit, that is, unable to grow in love.

19. Nor does it seem proved that souls in purgatory, at least not all of them, are certain and assured of their own salvation, even if we ourselves may be entirely certain of it.

20. Therefore, the pope, when he uses the words, "plenary remission of all penalties," does not actually mean "all penalties," but only those imposed by himself.

21. Thus, those indulgence preachers are in error who say that a man is absolved from every penalty and saved by papal indulgences.

22. As a matter of fact, the pope remits to souls in purgatory no penalty, which, according to canon law, they should have paid in their life.

23. If remission of all penalties whatsoever could be granted to anyone at all, certainly it would

be granted only to the most perfect, that is, to very few.

24. For this reason, most people are necessarily deceived by that indiscriminate and high-sounding promise of release from penalty.

25. That power which the pope has in general over purgatory corresponds to the power which any bishop or curate has in a particular way in his own diocese or parish.

26. The pope does very well when he grants remission to souls in purgatory, not but the power of the keys, which he does not have (i.e. does not extend to purgatory), but by way of intercession for them.

27. They preach only human doctrines who say that as soon as the money clinks into the money chest, the soul flies out of purgatory.

28. It is certain that when money clinks in the money chest, greed and avarice can be increased; but when the Church intercedes, the result is in the hands of God alone.

29. Who knows whether all souls in purgatory wish to be redeemed, since we have exceptions in St. Severinius and St. Paschal, as related in a legend? (i.e. Both of these popes desired to stay in purgatory longer than necessary to receive greater glory in heaven)

30. No one is sure of the integrity of his own contrition, much less of having received plenary remission.

31. The man who actually buys indulgences is as rare as he who is really penitent; indeed, he is exceedingly rare.

32. Those who believe that they can be certain of their salvation because they have indulgence letters will be eternally damned together with their teachers.

33. Men must be especially on their guard against those who say that the pope's pardons are that inestimable gift of God by which man is reconciled to him.

34. For the graces of indulgences are concerned only with the penalties of sacramental satisfaction established by man.

35. They who teach that contrition is not necessary on the part of those who intend to buy souls out of purgatory or to buy confessional privileges preach unchristian doctrine.

36. Any truly repentant Christian has the right to full remission of penalty and guilt, even without indulgence letters.

37. Any true Christian, whether living or dead, participates in all the blessings of Christ and the Church; and this is granted him by God, even without indulgence letters.

38. Nevertheless, papal remission and blessing are by no means to be disregarded, for they are, as I have said [Thesis 6], the proclamation of the divine remission.

39. It is very difficult, even for the most learned theologians, at one and the same time to

commend to the people the bounty of indulgences and the need for true contrition.

40. A Christian who is truly contrite seeks and loves to pay penalties for his sins; the bounty of indulgences, however, relaxes penalties and causes men to hate them-at least it furnishes occasion for hating them.

41. Papal indulgences must be preached with caution, lest people erroneously think that they are preferable to other good works of love.

42. Christians are to be taught that the pope does not intend that the buying of indulgences should in any way be compared with works of mercy.

43. Christians are to be taught that he who gives to the poor or lends to the needy does a better deed than he who buys indulgences.

44. Because love grows by works of love, man thereby becomes better. Man does not, however, become better by means of indulgences but is merely freed from penalties.

45. Christians are to be taught that he who sees a needy man and passes him by, yet gives his money for indulgences, does not buy papal indulgences but God's wrath.

46. Christians are to be taught that, unless they have more than they need they must reserve enough for their family needs and by no means squander it on indulgences.

47. Christians are to be taught that the buying of indulgences is a matter of free choice, not commanded.

48. Christians are to be taught that the pope, in granting indulgences, needs and thus desires their devout prayer more than their money.

49. Christians are to be taught that papal indulgences are useful only if they do not put their trust in them, but very harmful if they lose their fear of God because of them.

50. Christians are to be taught that if the pope knew the exactions of the indulgence preachers, he would rather that the basilica of St. Peter be burned to ashes than built up with the skin, flesh, and bones of his sheep.

51. Christians are to be taught that the pope would and should wish to give of his own money, even though he had to sell the basilica of St. Peter, to many of those from whom certain hawkers of indulgences cajole money.

52. It is vain to trust in salvation by indulgence letters, even though the indulgence commissary, or even the pope, was to offer his own soul as security.

53. They are enemies of Christ and the pope who forbid altogether the preaching of the Word of God in some Churches in order that indulgences may be preached in others.

54. Injury is done the Word of God when, in the same sermon an equal of larger amount of time is devoted to indulgences than to the Word.

55. It is certainly the pope's sentiment that if indulgences, which are a very insignificant thing, are celebrated with one bell, one procession, and in one ceremony, then the gospel, which is the very greatest thing, should be preached with a hundred bells, a hundred processions, and a hundred ceremonies.

56. The treasures of the Church out of which the pope distributes indulgences are not sufficiently discussed or known among the people of Christ.

57. That indulgences are not temporal treasures is certainly clear, for many [indulgence]preachers do not distribute them freely but only gather them.

58. Nor are they the merits of Christ and the saints, for, even without the pope, the latter always work grace for the inner man and the cross, death, and hell for the outer man.

59. St. Laurence said that the poor of the Church were the treasures of the Church, but he spoke according to the usage of the word in his own time.

60. Without want of consideration we say that the keys of the Church, given by the merits of Christ, are that treasure.

61. For it is clear that the pope's power is of itself sufficient for the remission of penalties and cases reserve by himself.

62. The true treasure of the Church is the most holy gospel of the glory and grace of God.

63. But this treasure is naturally most odious, for its males the first to be last. [Matthew 20:16]

64. On the other hand, the treasure of indulgences is naturally most acceptable for it makes the last to be first.

65. Therefore, the treasures of the gospel are nets with which one formerly fished for men of wealth.

66. The treasures of indulgences are nets with which one now fish for the wealth of men.

67. The indulgences, which the demagogue's acclaim as the greatest graces, are actually understood to be such only insofar as they promote gain.

68. They are nevertheless in truth the most insignificant graces when compared with the grace of God and the piety of the cross.

69. Bishops and curates are bound to admit the commissaries of papal indulgences with all reverence.

70. But they are much more bound to strain their eyes and ears lest these men preach their own dreams instead of what the pope has commissioned.

71. Let him who speaks against the truth concerning papal indulgences be anathema and accursed;

72. But let him who guards against the lust and license of the indulgence preachers be blessed;

73. Just as the pope justly thunders against those who by any means whatsoever contrive harm to the sale of indulgences,

74. But much more does he intend to thunder against those who use indulgences as a pretest to contrive him to holy love and truth.

75. To consider papal indulgences so great that they could absolve a man even if he had done the impossible and had violated the mother of God is madness.

76. We say on the contrary that papal indulgences cannot remove the very least of venial sins so far as guilt is concerned.

77. To say that even St. Peter, if he were now pope, could not grant greater graces is blasphemy against St. Peter and the pope.

78. We say on the contrary that even the present pope, or any pope whatsoever, has greater graces at his disposal, that is, the gospel, spiritual powers, gifts of healing, etc. as it is written in 1 Corinthians 12:28.

79. To say that the cross emblazoned with the papal coat of arms, and set up by the indulgence preachers, is equal in worth to the cross of Christ is blasphemy.

80. The bishops, curates, and theologians who permit such talk to be spread among the people will have to answer for this.

81. This unbridled preaching of indulgences makes it difficult even for learned men to rescue

the reverence, which is due the pope from slander or from the shrewd questions of the laity.

Theses # 83-89 use the same style of the repetitive use of "Again," which is then followed by a quoted statement.

83. Again, "Why are funeral and anniversary masses for the dead continued and why does he not return or permit the withdrawal of the endowments founded for them, since it is wrong to pray for the redeemed?"

84, Again, "What is this new piety of God and the pope that for a consideration of money they permit a man who is impious and their enemy to buy out of purgatory the pious soul of a friend of God and do not rather, because of the need of that pious and beloved soul, free it for pure love's sake?"

85. Again, "Why are the penitential canons, long since abrogated and dead in actual fact and through disuse, now satisfied by the granting of indulgences as though they were still alive and in force?"

86. Again, "Why does not the pope, whose wealth is today greater than the wealth of the richest Crassus, build this one basilica of St. Peter with his own money rather than with the money of the poor believers?"

87. Again, "What does the pope remit or grant to those who by perfect contrition already have a right to full remission and blessings?"

88. Again, "What greater blessing could come to the Church than if the pope were to bestow these remissions and blessings on every believer a hundred times a day, as he now does but once?"

89. "Since the pope seeks the salvation of the souls rather than money by indulgences, why does he suspend the indulgences and pardons previously granted when they have equal efficacy?"

Theses #90-95 are the Conclusion to Luther's argument that indulgences do not forgive; it is only the pope and the priests who have the authority to forgive sins.

90. To repress these very sharp arguments of the laity by force alone, and not to resolve them by giving reasons, is to expose the Church and the pope to the ridicule of their enemies and to make Christians unhappy.

91. If, therefore, indulgences were preached according to the spirit and intention of the pope, all these doubts would be readily resolved. Indeed, they would not exist.

92. Away then with all those prophets who say to the people of Christ, "Peace, peace," and there is no peace! [Jeremiah 6:14]

93. Blessed be all those prophets who say to the people of Christ, "Cross, cross," and there is no cross!

94. Christians should be exhorted to be diligent in following Christ, their head, through penalties, death, and hell;

95. And thus, be confident of entering into heaven through many tribulations rather than through the false security of peace. [Acts 14:22]

http://reverendluther.org/pdfs/The_Ninety-Five_Theses.pdf

# Appendix C

# The Schleitheim Confession

Although we don't have a complete confession of the Anabaptist movement, this was the document they used for the governance and leadership of the Church. It introduced a new understanding of how the true Church is a self-governing body. Until this time, groups had rebelled against Catholicism. Still, this statement got into the nitty gritty of how local Churches function, especially against the backdrop of State Religion. It indicated how a New Testament Church is supposed to function compared to Catholicism's mass.

The Schleitheim Confession was the most representative statement of Anabaptist principles by a group of Swiss Anabaptists in 1527 in Schleitheim, Switzerland. The real title is Brüderliche vereynigung etzlicher Kinder Gottes siben Artickel betreffend ... ("Brotherly Union of a Number of Children of God Concerning Seven Articles").

## Origin

The Confession is believed to have been written by Michael Sattler. The South German Ordnung of approximately the same date is similar to that of the Schleitheim Confession but contains many more Biblical references supporting the confession.: The Schleitheim confession continues to be a guide for Churches such as many Schwarzenau Brethren, the Bruderhof and the

Hutterites, who trace their spiritual heritage back to the Radical Reformation and the Anabaptists.

## Doctrine

The Confession consisted of seven articles, written during a time of severe persecution:

## Baptism

Baptism is administered only to those who have consciously repented, turned away from sin, amended their lives and believe that Christ has died for their sins and who request it for themselves (believer's baptism). Infant baptism is specifically denounced.

## The Ban (Excommunication)

A Christian should live with discipline and walk in the way of righteousness, following after Jesus every day. Those members of the Body who slip and fall into sin should be admonished twice in private, but the third offense should be openly disciplined and banned as a final recourse. This should always occur prior to the breaking of the bread, to preserve the unity and purity of the Body of Christ.

## Breaking of Bread (Communion)

Only those who have been baptized into the Body of Christ are members of the Body, thus only they can take part in the communion of the Body of Christ. Participation in Communion is an observance and remembrance of Christ's body and blood; the physical body and blood of Christ is not believed to be received in the sacrament.

## Separation from Evil

The community of Christians shall have no association with those who remain in disobedience and a spirit of rebellion against God. There can be no fellowship with the wickedness of this earthly world; therefore, there can be no participation in the organizations, works, Church services, meetings or civil affairs of those who live in contradiction to the commands of God (this may include Catholics and Protestants as well as other religions and pagans). All evil must be put away, including using weapons of force such as the sword and armor.

## Pastors in the Church

All elders and leaders in the Church must be men of good repute, as described in Scripture. Some of the responsibilities they must faithfully carry out are teaching, public reading of Scripture, disciplining, applying the ban, leading in prayer, and the sacraments. They are to be supported by the Church, but must also be disciplined if they sin.

## The Sword (Christian pacifism) – nonresistance

Violence must not be used in any circumstance. The way of nonviolence is patterned after the example of Christ who never exhibited violence in the face of persecution or as a punishment for sin. A Christian must love their enemies and pray for those who persecute them, as Jesus did. A Christian should not pass judgment in worldly disputes. It is not appropriate for a Christian to serve as a magistrate; a magistrate acts according to the rules of the world and uses force or orders force to be used, not acting according to the rules of heaven; their weapons are worldly, but the weapons of a Christian are spiritual.

### The Oath

No oaths should be taken because Jesus prohibited the taking of oaths and swearing, teaching rather complete honesty. Testifying or affirming is not the same thing as swearing. When a person bears testimony, they are testifying about the truth and the present, whether it be good or evil.

### The Schleitheim Confession,

https://courses.washington.edu/hist112/SCHLEITHEIM%20CONFESSION%20OF%20FAITH.htm

# Appendix D

# The Mayflower Compact

## November 11, 1620

This agreement of our first immigrants to the new land from England was the purpose of their coming to America. It was for the advancement of the Christian faith. This purpose was primary in their coming to America and fleeing oppression by the State Church, with the intent of having every citizen be a part of it. The statement settles the argument that the Pilgrims first came here, clearing up all myths contradicting this purpose. It also declares how worshiping the True God and believing in Christ's sacrifice for our sin was paramount and not a side issue can choose to be a part of or ignore it.

*IN THE NAME OF GOD, AMEN. We, whose names are underwritten, the Loyal Subjects of our dread Sovereign Lord King James, by the Grace of God, of Great Britain, France, and Ireland, King, Defender of the Faith, &c. Having undertaken for the Glory of God, and Advancement of the Christian Faith, and the Honors of our King and Country, a Voyage to plant the first Colony in the northern Parts of Virginia; Do by these Presents, solemnly and mutually, in the Presence of God and one another, covenant and combine ourselves together into a civil Body Politick, for our better Ordering and Preservation, and Furtherance of the Ends aforesaid: And by Virtue hereof do enact, constitute, and frame, such just and equal Laws,*

*Ordinances, Acts, Constitutions, and Officers, from time to time, as shall be thought most meet and convenient for the general Good of the Colony; unto which we promise all due Submission and Obedience.*

IN WITNESS whereof we have hereunto subscribed our names at Cape-Cod the eleventh of November, in the Reign of our Sovereign Lord King James, of England, France, and Ireland, the eighteenth, and of Scotland the fifty-fourth, Anno Domini; 1620

### Mayflower Society

https://themayflowersociety.org/history/the-mayflower-compact/

# Appendix E

# Amendment One to the Constitution of the United States

Since there are various opinions about the freedom Churches and Christians have in our country, it is good to look at the actual statement in this Constitution amendment and see its true intent.

It is important to remember that the amendment was heavily lobbied by John Leland (a Baptist Pastor) representing the Baptists and other groups who had been discriminated against by the Colonial official religion of Virginia: The Church of England. Their congregations were attacked, their pastors imprisoned, and baptismal services broke up. It was time to state clearly and concisely what the rights of true Christians were and what their freedoms entailed personally and in the churches, they were a part of.

## Amendment I to the Constitution of the United States

Congress shall make no law respecting an establishment of religion, or prohibiting the free exercise thereof; or abridging the freedom of speech, or of the press; or the right of the people peaceably to assemble, and to petition the Government for a redress of grievances.

# The First Amendment of the United States Constitution:

## Freedom of Religion

The simple statement means Congress cannot make laws that ***establish a religion*** or ***prohibit the free exercise of religion***

This means there will be no state Church favoring one denomination. It also means Christians can share what they believe and seek to lead others to that faith anytime, anywhere, without restriction.

Taken in this respect, the statement throws a new light on those who say the Churches freedom ends at the back door of the Church and is under the regulation of the government, primarily to muzzle their right of free speech when they leave its confines.

https://www.archives.gov/contact

National Archives: America's Founding Documents

*Bill of Rights: A Transcription*

# Appendix F

# Roosevelt's Prayer

President Franklin Delano Roosevelt gave this prayer on D. Day, June 6, 1945, when the Allied troops stormed the beaches of Normandy.

The prayer is unique because it is the last prayer ever heard by a President of the United States on national television. Here it is in its entirety:

"My fellow Americans: Last night, when I spoke with you about the fall of Rome, I knew at that moment that troops of the United States and our allies were crossing the Channel in another and greater operation. It has come to pass with success thus far.

And so, in this poignant hour, I ask you to join with me in prayer:

Almighty God: Our sons, pride of our Nation, this day have set upon a mighty endeavor, a struggle to preserve our Republic, our religion, and our civilization, and to set free a suffering humanity.

Lead them straight and true; give strength to their arms, stoutness to their hearts, steadfastness in their faith.

They will need Thy blessings. Their road will be long and hard. For the enemy is strong. He may hurl back our forces. Success may not come with rushing speed, but we shall return again and again;

and we know that by Thy grace, and by the righteousness of our cause, our sons will triumph.

They will be sore tried, by night and by day, without rest-until the victory is won. The darkness will be rent by noise and flame. Men's souls will be shaken with the violences of war.

For these men are lately drawn from the ways of peace. They fight not for the lust of conquest. They fight to end conquest. They fight to liberate. They fight to let justice arise, and tolerance and good will among all Thy people. They yearn but for the end of battle, for their return to the haven of home.

Some will never return. Embrace these, Father, and receive them, Thy heroic servants, into Thy kingdom.

And for us at home -- fathers, mothers, children, wives, sisters, and brothers of brave men overseas -- whose thoughts and prayers are ever with them--help us, Almighty God, to rededicate ourselves in renewed faith in Thee in this hour of great sacrifice.

Many people have urged that I call the Nation into a single day of special prayer. But because the road is long and the desire is great, I ask that our people devote themselves in a continuance of prayer. As we rise to each new day, and again when each day is spent, let words of prayer be on our lips, invoking Thy help to our efforts.

Give us strength, too—strength in our daily tasks, to redouble the contributions we make in the physical and the material support of our armed forces.

And let our hearts be stout, to wait out the long travail, to bear sorrows that may come, to impart our courage unto our sons wheresoever they may be.

And, O Lord, give us Faith. Give us Faith in Thee; Faith in our sons; Faith in each other; Faith in our united crusade. Let not the keenness of our spirit ever be dulled. Let not the impacts of temporary events, of temporal matters of but fleeting moment let not these deter us in our unconquerable purpose.

With Thy blessing, we shall prevail over the unholy forces of our enemy. Help us to conquer the apostles of greed and racial arrogancies. Lead us to the saving of our country, and with our sister Nations into a world unity that will spell a sure peace a peace invulnerable to the scheming's of unworthy men. And a peace that will let all of men live in freedom, reaping the just rewards of their honest toil.

Thy will be done, Almighty God.

Amen."

**This text was originally published by the Franklin Delano Roosevelt Presidential Library & Museum.**

# Index of People, Places, and Words

# About the Author

Dan Nelson is an author who writes about Baptist History and Practice. He served as an ordained Baptist pastor of three churches for the last 50 years. He and his wife, Janice, live in Live Oak, Texas. They recently moved after spending four years in Sherwood, Oregon, when Dan retired from a 35-year full-time pastorate at First Baptist Church of Camarillo, California.

Dan writes and contributes various articles to Baptist History groups while serving as an administrator of an online Bible Study group. He has taught the History of Christianity at Channel Islands Bible College and is the author of six other books. Dan also preaches and teaches at various churches on Baptist History and Doctrine. He remains active through supply preaching. He also teaches classes at his home church, First Baptist Church of Universal City, Texas, on Baptist History and Practice using two of his books for reference.

Dan's most recent books continue his theme of seeking to write on Baptist History and biographies that cover the establishment and continuous story of Baptists. His ambition of writing on ongoing Baptist History was his motivation for his previous books on Baptist Biographies and Happenings in America and his book on Early Baptists: A Comparative History of the Anabaptist and English Baptist Movements. Early Baptists is his most extensive and challenging work. It covers two centuries with many biographies, doctrinal explanations, and historical events in these groups during the Reformation era and the turbulent seventeenth century religious conflict in England.

Dan's new book: Nelson's Notes on Christian History: From New Testament Christianity to the Present Day is a completed expansion of his original Christian History outline when he taught for several years at Channel Islands Bible College. He has adapted the outline to book form and added a massive number of references and information from his original outline over twenty years ago. Each chapter is a balanced account of Christian History through the ages in a chronological manner. He designed the book to be simple enough for the layman to understand while still being a scholarly work.

The book will give a good handle on the flow of Christian happenings, biographies and turning points from the New Testament to the present day. The work is highly informational and can be used in research to find out more about these subjects while illuminating on these truths without being bogged down in minutia. The book will give concise information while answering many questions and offering sources to follow-up on the subject.

Dan's book Baptist Revival 2.0 Baptist Faith and Practice Analyzed and Explained Scripturally and Historically is a deeper understanding of Baptist beliefs and practice from his first book: Baptist Revival Reaffirming Baptist Principles in Today's Changing Church Scene. It gives a historical background of how Baptist beliefs were courageous and purposeful in Christian History.

The content is a compilation of a series of articles Dan shared on various Baptist History groups in various social media venues. The quotes and understanding of what Baptists believed are explored from every angle. Dan hopes the information in this book can be used in teaching venues in churches and schools so that the appendices condense the book's content for this very purpose.

A Burning and Shining Light was his biography of George Whitefield, the Great Awakening Preacher who led the Awakening Movement in England and America. This book was a product of many years of research with his Ph. D dissertation on the First Great Awakening Leaders and their preaching styles. The biography was listed in Amazon's "Hot New Releases" of the History Section after its first week of publication. Dan also does a dramatic monologue and sermon excerpts on Whitefield dressed as Whitefield.

Dan's first two books deal with diverse subjects. Baptist Revival: Reaffirming Baptist Principles in Today's Changing Church Scene gives a concise understanding of some of the beliefs and practices that have made Baptists unique, with Scripture and history to support his writing.

Game on All the Time: Growing up in the Home of a Legendary Football Coach is a fun book recounting Dan's Father, a High School Football Coach in the South. He relates locker room stories, an account of his dad's life, with many interesting stories about family and community that abound with much humor.

Dan holds a Doctor of Ministry degree from Southwestern Baptist Theological Seminary in Fort Worth, Texas, a Doctor of Philosophy degree from California Graduate School of Theology in Glendale, California, a Master of Divinity degree from New Orleans Baptist Theological Seminary in New Orleans, Louisiana and attended Golden Gate Baptist Theological Seminary in Mill Valley, California. He graduated from William Carey University in Hattiesburg, Mississippi, with a B.A. degree.

Dan and his wife Janice have two daughters, Krista and Kimberly, who live with their families in San Antonio, Texas, close to Dan and Janice. Dan has served on the Board of Trustees at Southwestern Baptist Theological Seminary in Fort Worth, Texas, and as National Alumni Chairman for New Orleans Baptist Theological Seminary. He served as President of the California Southern Baptist Pastor's Conference in 2002.

www.ingramcontent.com/pod-product-compliance
Lightning Source LLC
Chambersburg PA
CBHW051809150726
47998CB00001B/76